Praying Alone and Together

An 11-Session Prayer Module
for Small Faith Communities

Arthur R. Baranowski

With Kathleen M. O'Reilly
and Carrie M. Piro

Nihil Obstat: Rev. Hilarion Kistner, O.F.M.
Rev. Robert L. Hagedorn

Imprimi Potest: Rev. Jeremy Harrington, O.F.M.
Provincial

Imprimatur: +James H. Garland, V.G.
Archdiocese of Cincinnati
August 22, 1988

Scripture citations are taken from *The New
American Bible With Revised New Testament,*
copyright ©1986 by the Confraternity of Christian
Doctrine, and are used by permission. All rights
reserved.

Book and cover design by Julie Lonneman.

ISBN 0-86716-897-8

©1988, Arthur R. Baranowski
All rights reserved
Published by St. Anthony Messenger Press
Printed in the U.S.A.

Preface

This book provides everything necessary for a small-group
prayer workshop. Each person will need his or her own
copy, since the book consists mainly of activity sheets and
prayer exercises to be worked through—and written
on—together in a group session or alone between
sessions.

This workshop is organized around 11 group
Sessions—ideally spaced two weeks apart. An
introductory page for each Session gives an overview of
what is to be done "Together: For the Session" as well as
"Alone: Until the Next Session." Activity Sheets for group
use can be found immediately after this overview page.

Beginning with Session 4, seven prayer exercises are
provided for praying alone between Sessions. These
follow immediately after each Session's Activity Sheets. An
Introduction explaining how to use these Prayer Times
can be found on page 20.

Facilitator's Notes are included in a special section
beginning on page 85. No special expertise is needed to
lead a group through this workshop. Some groups may
even wish to rotate facilitators for various Sessions. The
person organizing this prayer workshop or facilitating the
group for any particular Session should read the
introduction to these Notes.

A primary goal of *Praying Alone and Together* is to
help parishes restructure into smaller base churches
through the Called to Be Church process. (This process is
explained in the book *Creating Small Faith Communities:
A Plan for Restructuring Your Parish and Renewing
Catholic Life* from St. Anthony Messenger Press.) This
workshop is called a Prayer Module because it serves as
one component of this larger process. But it can also be
used independently of this program. It does work best,
however, when a group has already had an opportunity to
get to know each other through RENEW or some other
small group process.

Contents

What Is Prayer?

Together: For the Session

Purpose

To articulate some definitions of prayer
To identify present prayer habits
To notice past and present influences on prayer life

Activity Sheets

1. Personal Prayer
2. Identifying Prayer Activities
3. Evaluating Prayer Activities
4. Many Paths, One Journey
5. Reflecting on 'Many Paths, One Journey'

See Facilitator's Notes, p. 88

Alone: Until Next Session

Choose the kind of prayer which you find most satisfying and spend 10 minutes praying in that way each day. Begin making any changes in your prayer that you decided upon as a result of this Session.

Write in your journal specific descriptions of any difficulties which you have in prayer.

Activity Sheet 1

Personal Prayer

Be as specific as possible as you respond to each item.

1. Defining Prayer: What is *prayer* — to *you*?

2. Recognizing Your Present Prayer Habits: When do you pray? (Times of trouble? Happy times?) How often? At what time of the day do you pray? How do you pray? (Memorized prayers? Prayer book? Your own words? Quiet listening?)

3. Recalling Your Prayer Roots: Who taught you to pray? What is your earliest memory of praying? Name any person who has inspired you to take your relationship with God seriously.

Activity Sheet 2

Identifying Prayer Activities

List on the lines below any activities which you call prayer. Use enough words to describe clearly each kind of prayer. For example: "I say the Our Father and the Hail Mary," and, "I talk to God spontaneously during the day."

Fill in the columns after each activity as follows:

In Column A, estimate how often you do the activity each week.

In Column B, rate from 1 to 4 how important each activity is to you. (1 = most important; 4 = least important.)

In Column C, note when this prayer activity began in your life. (C indicates childhood, M middle part of life, R for recently.)

	A *How often?*	B *How important?*	C *When begun?*

Activity Sheet 3

Evaluating Prayer Activities

Use your responses to the chart on Activity Sheet 2 as the basis for answering these questions:

1. What prayer activity do you do most often? Why?

2. What determines how often you pray?

3. Which of your prayer activities are more satisfying to you? What makes these more satisfying?

4. Who taught or encouraged you to pray? Has your prayer changed since childhood? If so, how? If not, why not?

Sum up your reflections on prayer so far by completing the following sentences:

1. What I have learned about myself from this prayer assessment is:

2. This is the change I would recommend to myself:

Activity Sheet 4

Many Paths, One Journey

Prayer brings us closer to God. All the different kinds of prayer are only different paths we take on one journey—a journey toward union with God.

Growing closer to God, like growing closer to anyone else, requires that we get to know God the way God really is, not the way we try to make him—or her—to be. Getting to know any person means we need to listen as well as to talk.

God wants me to know him. God wants to reveal himself. I need to listen. I also need to take time for reflection in order to discover what God is showing to me.

Then, I must respond. I talk back. I ask. I thank. I say I am sorry. Or I praise. As I do this my life begins to change. As I am growing in love of God, I grow in my love for people and the world.

Prayer begins in listening to God. How does God speak? Through Scripture, the church, the sacraments. Yet God also speaks in every aspect of life—art, politics, play—even sin. Everything and everybody can be a source of prayer if I listen—if I am present to God's communication in everything.

Listening takes discipline. It is work to be present to someone and to hear what is *really* being said. Notice how a mother can sometimes understand what her child is really saying by hearing between the sounds of the words. She can pick up how her child feels even though those feelings are not expressed in the words. Time and attention given to her child enable her to be quite sensitive to any communication.

Sensitivity to God's communication also grows slowly through time and practice. In that communication I must let go of much of my self-centeredness and my narrow ways of seeing things. To get beyond myself and open up to God requires that I persevere in prayer.

Beginners in prayer often enjoy a feeling of God's closeness. Later, however, they sometimes experience little or no feeling of God's consoling presence. In fact, God may seem to be totally absent. Some people even feel what Jesus felt on the cross when he asked God why God had abandoned him.

We pray, then, not to get good feelings, but to offer our faith and trust. If we continue to pray, then we will begin to find God in a new and purified way. We will eventually turn a corner to find God very much present to us again.

At the Second Vatican Council, the church reminded us that each person is called to holiness. Know that *you* are called to a deep union with God. Not only is this closeness with God possible, it is *God's* very desire. It is you—with your temperament, your strengths, your weaknesses, your background, your scars—that God calls. God will lead you into a close relationship—if you allow it.

Activity Sheet 5

Reflecting on 'Many Paths, One Journey'

1. What made sense to you about prayer in the essay on Activity Sheet 4? What did not?

2. Why the title "Many Paths, One Journey"?

3. The essay points out that God is communicating in all of the events of life. Do most people see God communicating in the happenings of life? Do you? Why or why not?

4. Can all of life be a prayer without taking any specific quiet times to reflect? Are you a reflective person? Do you need to grow in this way? Explain.

Who Is God?

Together: For the Session

Purpose

To become aware of personal images of God

To move toward a stronger personal relationship with God

Activity Sheets

6. Describing God
7. Discovering the God Behind the Images
8. Growing in Prayer

See Facilitator's Notes, pp. 88-90

Alone: Until Next Session

Recall each evening the gifts of the day and write a prayer of thanks in your journal.

Activity Sheet 6

Describing God

How we feel about God flows from our images of God. Check the phrases below which are close to your own sense of God.

☐ interested in me
☐ a powerful force behind everything
☐ someone I have an obligation to
☐ the onlooker
☐ close
☐ someone to bargain with
☐ reliable
☐ someone to argue with
☐ one who has the answers
☐ a vague presence

☐ almighty
☐ unreal, doesn't exist
☐ someone to stay on good terms with
☐ someone who saves me
☐ someone I enjoy being with
☐ someone involved in my life
☐ someone to be careful of
☐ someone who teaches me
☐ someone far away
☐ _____(other)

Look over the phrases you chose. Some descriptions may be more accurate for you than others. Circle those which *best* describe your experience of God. Using these words or phrases, write a description of *your* God.

Activity Sheet 7

Discovering the God Behind the Images

On Activity Sheet 6, you checked words which describe God for you. Using the categories below, go back to Activity Sheet 6 and decide where your images fall. Place a D for distant, an A for authoritative or a P for personal before each checked item.

Distant	*Authoritative*	*Personal*
almighty	someone to be careful of	someone to stay on good terms with
someone far away	someone I have an obligation to	interested in me
a vague presence	one who has the answers	close
an onlooker	someone to bargain with	someone I enjoy being with
a powerful force behind everything	someone to argue with	involved in my life
unreal, doesn't exist	someone who teaches me	reliable

Drawing on what you have learned from doing Activity Sheets 6 and 7, write a sentence or two on "The God to whom I pray (or to whom I am unable to pray)."

Activity Sheet 8

Growing in Prayer

1. Describe in detail your favorite way of praying. Mention the place you pray, your posture, your feelings. What brings you to prayer? (Anxiety? Gratitude? Suffering?)

2. What clues does the above description give about the God to whom you are praying? Write down as many descriptive words as possible.

3. Do you notice any change in your image of God over the years? If so, what is changed? How did it come about?

4. Name a way in which you would like to grow in your understanding and experience of God. How can you develop toward that goal?

Relating Faith and Prayer

Together: For the Session

Purpose

To understand prayer as an act of faith

To appreciate and understand faith as essential to prayer

Activity Sheets

9. Faith and Prayer
10. Growing in Faith
11. Moving Mountains

See Facilitator's Notes, pp. 90-91

Alone: Until Next Session

Find some time each day for some kind of prayer and reflection. Try a different way of praying on some days. For example, prepare for prayer with a breathing or other relaxation exercise or place yourself in a Gospel story.

Activity Sheet 9

Faith and Prayer

Faith is a response to an invitation from God. God invites me. God acts first. I respond; but even as I do, it is still God who leads. Letting God lead means that I give up some control in my life.

Christian faith is not a belief in a God "up there" who made everything a long time ago and now watches life go on by itself. Faith in the God of Jesus holds that God is near, caring and active in my life.

Faith tells me that God loves me, that I am lovable. Even my basic attitude about myself can change because of my faith in God.

Can doubts, or a questioning attitude, be compatible with faith? Yes. Faith can live with questions and continue to ask them. But faith also trusts God unconditionally—even when things don't make sense, or when God does not seem to be present, or when God's presence doesn't seem to make any difference.

Faith trusts God enough to believe in the truths God reveals. We find many of these truths in the teachings of our community, the church. God also asks faith in other truths, however: the truth about myself—that I am God's creation uniquely and lovably made; the truth about the human race—that human beings are made in God's image, have rights that are to be respected, and are worthy of our best efforts; the truth about the world—that it is God's creation which needs to be reverenced and freed from the things and the greedy persons which destroy it.

Faith is, then, not a separate piece of life; it is a window through which I see everything else. Faith also spurs me to action and to a particular style of life.

I relate to God with my own personality. I relate as *I* am, not as someone else is. If I'm a low-key, reliable, hardworking type, then I will relate to God in this way. And it will be different from the way a poetic or highly sensitive person will relate. *My* relationship with God is one of a kind.

Any close relationship, including one with God, re-forms a person. Growing in faith and in prayer will bring about changes in me.

Activity Sheet 10

Growing in Faith

1. Faith develops through the stages of life. How is your faith the same and how different from childhood to the present?

       From teen years to the present?

       From 10 years ago to the present?

2. Has your faith in God had an influence on your life in the past few days? How?

3. Explain how a person can have faith and still have questions. Give an example from your life or someone else's.

Activity Sheet 11

Moving Mountains

"If you have faith the size of a mustard seed, you will say to this mountain, 'Move from here to here' and it will move. Nothing shall be impossible for you." (Matthew 17:20)

Jesus was not speaking of moving actual mountains. Jesus speaks figuratively to make his point: Faith has the power to change the landscape of our lives. Faith is *powerful*.

Countless believers have shown how the power of faith in their lives can remove obstacles. People have done great things—way beyond anything they would be capable of on their own. Faith has kept people alive and hopeful even in the face of great tragedy. Only through faith have some endured great temptation. Some have made mistakes and failed miserably but, because of faith, had the courage to start over.

1. How would you explain Matthew 17:20 to someone who claims to have no faith?

2. Recall a difficult experience in your recent life. Did you approach God to help you deal with the situation? How? What was your prayer like?

S E S S I O N 4

Sharpening Prayer Skills

Together: For the Session

Purpose

To evaluate personal listening skills
To discover and practice techniques for better listening

Activity Sheets

12. Listening Skills
13. How Society Affects Listening
14. Personal Barriers to Listening
15. Improving Listening Skills

See Facilitator's Notes, pp. 91-93

Alone: Until Next Session

Prayer Times

Introduction to Prayer Times
1. Just Be Yourself
2. God
3. You and God
4. Who, Me?
5. The Other Side of You
6. You Again!
7. Prayer: A Duty or a Privilege?

Also

Practice listening skills with someone each day, applying the rules on Activity Sheet 15.

Activity Sheet 12

Listening Skills

Listening to other people:

1. I know I am a *(choose one)* ☐ good ☐ poor ☐ mediocre listener because

2. I listen best when

3. I choose not to listen sometimes when

4. I think active listening (that is, working to hear both the speaker's words *and* the feelings behind the words) is ☐ easy ☐ hard because

Listening to God:

1. I listen best when

2. I know I am a *(choose one)* ☐ good ☐ poor ☐ mediocre listener because

3. I choose not to listen sometimes when

4. I think active listening is ☐ easy ☐ hard because

Activity Sheet 13

How Society Affects Listening

Work with other members of your small group in completing this activity.

1. The way we live together in today's world does not encourage listening—except on the surface. List the obstacles around us that make real (active) listening difficult.

2. Think of the kinds of communities people live in and work in. Consider the way we travel. Look at how our educational system affects us. Consider family life: One study, for instance, showed that the average time that American parents spend with their children is 20 minutes per day. How does this affect our ability to listen to God?

3. What can we do to hear God better in today's world?

Activity Sheet 14

Personal Barriers to Listening

We all have barriers within ourselves that keep us from listening to others. As you read the following, check items which describe your barriers. It may help to keep in mind a person to whom you find it difficult to listen.

☐ Self-interest and past experience condition me not to pay attention.

☐ I tend to make assumptions about what the other person is going to say.

☐ I do not like what I hear.

☐ I do not like the person who is speaking.

☐ I am in an anxiety-producing situation.

☐ Certain words trigger emotional responses such as anger or defensiveness.

☐ I tune out people who have poor delivery.

☐ I feel that a certain person has nothing valuable to say.

☐ I tend to use my listening time to compose my rebuttal.

☐ Cultural or social differences trigger stereotyping.

☐ Others?

Look over each of the barriers and see how it could affect your listening to God. Then consider the following examples of how societal and personal barriers may combine and further affect our listening:

• If I am a middle-class American constantly urged to want bigger and better things, might I seriously block hearing the Lord's call to a simpler life-style?

• If I am poor, can my desire to have more things for myself keep me from sharing what I do have or from working toward good for everyone?

• Or does the information glut, the amount of words thrown at me throughout the day, make it difficult to focus on what is really important?

• Can you think of more examples?

Activity Sheet 15

Improving Listening Skills

Read and reread the following. As you spend time with various people throughout the coming weeks, put some of these rules and guidelines into practice.

Listening is a skill. We develop a skill by practice. The following rules and attitudes for active listening can be practiced with a spouse, child, parent, friend, coworker.

Definitions

active listening: careful attention to both *content* and *feeling*

content: what the words mean

feeling: how the person is feeling (angry? frustrated? curious? afraid? joyful? sad? confused?)

Rules

1. Listen between the lines. Try to pick up both the content and how the person feels about his or her position.

2. Try not to anticipate what the other is getting at.

3. Do not form conclusions or begin to construct your reply until you have listened to the end and understood the other's position.

4. Pause and consider what you have heard before replying.

5. Assume you probably don't understand completely; ask for feedback on what you think you heard.

Attitudes

1. Care about other people. Be concerned with how they feel.

2. Assume the other person has value and something to offer.

3. Assume everyone is unique. Accept each person as unique. If the person you are listening to has had an experience similar to yours, it does not mean that you know how he or she feels. Listen for the other person's feelings, not your own.

4. Empathize. Understand how the other person feels. (This is different from sympathize, which means feeling the same thing.)

Introduction to Prayer Times

A relationship with God grows the way any relationship grows—by communication. Prayer is our communication with God. Prayer, like any dialogue, involves listening, noticing, responding and a willingness to reconsider one's values and perceptions. But prayer is also just *being with* God, being aware of his—or her—presence.

Ability to communicate develops by practice. We need to pray more than we need to discuss prayer. So until the end of the Prayer Module, you are asked to set aside at least 10 minutes each day for prayer. Prayer Times will offer a variety of prayer exercises that you can try. Further support for your growth in prayer will come from the sharing of prayer experiences in the group.

Many people find morning the best time for prayer; praying at the start of the day opens us to recognize the events and persons of the day as "God incidents." But others prefer a midday break or a period in the evening. Choose a time which is good for you, realistically assessing your commitments and your unique personality.

Each Prayer Time format includes four R's:

Relating: an instruction or a thought-starter.

Reflecting and Recording: an opportunity to write down your own experience on a particular topic.

Responding: a suggested word or action from you in response to God's communication.

Remembering: a practical way to carry your prayer throughout the other hours of the day.

Various Prayer Times will take different amounts of time to complete. So do not obligate yourself to one exercise each day. Taking a specified time each day to pray—such as 10 minutes—is much more important than completing these exercises.

In most cases you will have more days between your group Sessions than there are exercises. (Seven Prayer Times follow each Session.) You may stay with one exercise for two or three days—or an entire week. Or you might decide to repeat some of the Prayer Times. And some days you might wish to pray in another way.

Many of the prayer formats may be new to you. If you are open, you will find new ways in which God can speak to you. After you try the newer ways of praying, you may want to use some of them throughout your life for prayer. Others you may later decide to discard because they are not comfortable for your personality.

As you begin these Prayer Times, know that God is waiting and wants to give greater fullness of life to you.

Prayer Time 1

Just Be Yourself

Relating

We all act a certain way with people. We want people to think of us a certain way, to have a particular image of us. Usually we do let some people know us better.

Who knows you best? List the people in order starting with best, second best and so on.

Why can you be yourself with these people?

Communication with God happens when I am myself with him. I have to be myself. The person I am is the person God speaks to and chooses. I can respond to God only as myself with whatever feelings I feel.

That's who I am and that's the person God speaks to.

We can be tempted to say, "I'm not the religious type," or, "I can't pray. I've got too many bad habits." But we can and must pray as we are. To constantly compare ourselves to someone else or to think that we have to say certain things to God will hinder prayer. There are no experts in prayer. We each will find the way which will be God's way for us.

20

Reflecting and Recording

Describe yourself in a few sentences as honestly as you can. Use single words or phrases, but say what makes you the person you are—hard-working, a quick temper, good humor, on the lazy side and so on.

Write a sentence about what you do not find attractive about God. Write anything that comes to mind, such as God's seeming vagueness, God's ways not being understandable, God's judgment and so on.

Responding

Sit erect, but relax your body. Take a breath and feel it flow through your body. Close your eyes and breathe several times, each time a bit more deeply—without forcing it. After this breathing, become aware of God choosing you to become closer to him. Stay with this. If time allows, try to choose God by appreciating some quality God has.

Write some response to God.

Remembering

In Christ the fullness of [God]
  resides in bodily form. (Colossians 2:9)

Look for a quality of God you admire as it shows itself today: for example, good humor or consideration in persons you work with, the beauty of nature, a wise statement, someone's forgiveness, the little things in a day. Take the odd moments of the day to notice a quality of God.

Prayer Time 2

God

Relating

Who is God? Is it possible to know God? Does God ever really let us know him (or her!)?

God wants to be known, loved, appreciated. The great communication of God is his Son, Jesus Christ. Jesus is God in a human way we can understand.

Our knowledge of God is clearest when we listen to his Son who is divine but also fully and completely human—one of us forever. In Jesus, God is not distant and untouchable.

God is all-powerful, almighty, all-knowing. But God is also the baby who was born, the child reared in Nazareth, the man tempted in the desert, the teacher hung on a cross. And God is also the man raised up from the dead and fully alive. In Jesus, God is with us now!

This same God appreciates knowing me. This same God wants me to know him, not in some vague spiritual way, but concretely—in Jesus.

Reflecting and Recording

Complete this sentence: What I appreciate most about God is...

Responding

[God] blew into his nostrils the breath of life.
  (Genesis 2:7)

Put down your pen. Close your eyes. Sit erect. Pay attention to your breathing. Take as long as you need to be relaxed and centered on your breath. Imagine God breathing into you with each inhalation. Relax in God's presence. Be yourself with God for a minute or so.

Offer a response that comes from you. You may, for instance, want to ask for the grace to accept yourself honestly. Write your response.

Remembering

As you are forced to wait during the day—in traffic, on the commuter train, in line, between things—take a moment to be yourself with God.

Prayer Time 3

You and God

Relating

We must be ourselves with God. We must also let God be God. That means we will not always understand God right away. Sometimes we will misunderstand God and make the mistake of limiting God by *our* images and attributing to God *our* thoughts. We all try to reduce God to our level. That's normal.

As we stay with the journey of prayer each day, however, God will be doing most of the communicating. So we will come to know him better and come to know ourselves better, too. God is communicating all the time in our lives.

St. Augustine lived a long time before he realized that God was speaking to him. Before he recognized God, Augustine lived with a woman for years, had an illegitimate son and joined a weird sect. In the book we now call *The Confessions of St. Augustine*, he writes:

Late have I loved you, O Beauty ever ancient, ever new, late have I loved you! You were within me, but I was outside, and it was there that I searched for you. In my unloveliness I plunged into the lovely things which you created. You were with me, but I was not with you. Created things kept me from you, yet if they had not been in you they would not have been at all. You called, you shouted, and you broke through my deafness.

Reflecting and Recording

God is seeking a friendship with you. This relationship is possible for you. Write your reaction to this possibility in a sentence or two.

List a few qualities you consider important for any friendship.

Which of these qualities do you bring to any friendship?

Can you name one quality you have that hinders a friendship?

Responding

Reread Augustine's words slowly. Think about each activity and person of this day. Can you allow each of this day's activities and each person to be an expression of God's desire for friendship with you? What will you allow to be an expression of God's friendship today?

Remembering

Take the spare moment, the breather, the 30 seconds before the next event to see in the things and people around you a call to friendship with the Lord.

Prayer Time 4

Who, Me?

Relating

As Catholics we believe that God speaks to us even if we haven't gotten around to listening on a daily basis. Often it's not until we experience a major crisis—like cancer, the death of a loved one, a shattered marriage—that we then turn to God for a strength or a peace we can't give ourselves.

In our everyday lives, however, we can forget to develop our friendship with God. We get busy and, most of the time, just handle our own lives. These Prayer Times focus on these ordinary times and help us see God in the day-by-day lives we lead.

"What's the angle?" "Where's the catch?" This cautious cynicism is so much a part of survival in our day-to-day world that we can tend to keep our distance from God the way we do with people. But God is not after anything. God simply wants to be a person who makes a difference in our lives. God is seeking a friendship with each of us. And, as in any friendship, both parties must trust each other's intentions and believe the offer is sincere.

Why me? Why you? We don't know. We simply accept the fact that God chooses us and invites us to be his friends. We must simply trust his call to relationship.

Reflecting and Recording

Write your reaction to the fact that God wants you for a friend.

If you can, name a time in your life when friendship with God or Jesus had meaning for you.

Why did you begin this Prayer Module?

23

Responding

> The LORD called me from birth,
> from my mother's womb he gave me my name.
> (Isaiah 49:1)

Take a few moments simply to be in God's presence. One way to do this is to close your eyes, sit erect and image the center of your body (wherever you imagine that center to be). Let your center become quiet and peaceful. Now accept God there in your center. Be with God awhile. Let God say your name. Let God call your name. Stay present to this call as long as you are able.

Write a response if you wish.

Remembering

Take a spare moment to let yourself hear the Lord call your name with affection. Notice your name being called by others throughout the day. Is God also calling your name at these times?

Reflecting and Recording

What do I like least about myself?

What makes it difficult for me to accept that part of myself?

Prayer Time 5

The Other Side of You

(This Prayer Time can be extended over several days and repeated again and again.)

Relating

A study of people who underwent plastic surgery for serious facial deformities reveals an important truth about self-esteem. Even though scars, distorted noses and misshapen lips were transformed to create greatly improved faces—beautiful faces—the physical change made little difference in people's self-esteem. The study showed that we accept and like ourselves or we don't. Physical appearance has little to do with it.

Self-esteem is a struggle for most of us, at least at times. Whether or not I like myself influences my ability to make friends because friendship begins in trusting that the other person genuinely likes me. I have to believe I'm likeable as I am—warts and all.

Yet we find it hard to reveal our "warts" to others. All of us have parts that we find unpleasant to face, parts we don't even want to look at ourselves. That "shadow side" holds pain, embarrassment, limitations, fears and desires.

Responding

> Yet it was our infirmities that he bore,
> our sufferings that he endured....
> [B]y his stripes we were healed. (Isaiah 53:4-5)

Sit erect. Let your body relax by mentally letting go of all your tension. Begin letting go in the soles of your feet and work your way up through your legs and back and neck. Go all the way up to the scalp. It may be helpful to close your eyes as you do this.

In your imagination, slowly walk up the hill of Calvary. Feel the hot day and the effort needed to climb the hill. Begin to walk through the crowd of men, women and children, all laughing, poking fun and enjoying the suffering of the man on the cross. Notice Jesus convulsing with pain, embarrassed by his own nakedness. Hear the words: Our sufferings he endured.

Jesus is turning his head toward you. Your eyes meet. Tell him what you like least about yourself and give him that. Make sure you do give him that part of yourself.

Remembering

Memorize the above Scripture quote from Isaiah, or write it out to keep with you. Refer to these words throughout the day.

Prayer Time 6

You Again!

(This Prayer Time can be extended over several days and repeated again and again.)

Relating

The last Prayer Time called you to be yourself with God. The prayer encouraged getting in touch with some part of yourself that you don't particularly like. Why tell God about that? Doesn't God already know that about you? Yes, but telling God about ourselves helps us be ourselves with God. We tell God for the sake of our relationship, not for God's sake. We need to share hard truths—and still trust him to love us.

Sharing a part of ourselves that is not pleasing, or which is embarrassingly painful, lets God be our best friend. Not only does God do what a friend does by continuing to love us, but God takes upon himself our pain! "Yet it was our infirmities that he bore...." (Isaiah 53:4) *Our* infirmities! *My* infirmities! Stay with that thought awhile. Write a sentence or two of reaction.

Reflecting and Recording

Being ourselves with God means coming to prayer with the feelings we have at that particular time, whatever the feelings—joy, hostility, aggravation, self-disgust.

Some pious Catholics or "born-again" Christians can seem so controlled, so sweet or uplifted. But being real is more important than being perfect. When we do not feel good about ourselves, we tend to withdraw from communication with people who love us—and from God. So when we need to trust God's faithfulness the most, we withdraw. But there is no feeling or mood that cannot be brought to prayer. You can be and feel anything and still pray. Prayer is a come-as-you-are activity.

Recall a time when you disliked yourself. How did you feel? What did you do?

Could you bring yourself before God in that situation today?

Responding

Today's prayer is about Peter the Apostle and the Peter in us. Peter loved Jesus and said so with loud protests many, many times in front of the other apostles. Peter meant what he said. Peter, however, was sometimes a coward and a braggart. He often faltered: He sank in coming to Jesus on the water; he fell asleep when Jesus needed him in the Garden of Gethsamane; he misunderstood Jesus' words. Finally, Peter denied Jesus three times after protesting the night before that he would never desert his Lord.

The Scripture quoted below is Christ's conversation with Peter after the Resurrection. Peter, definitely not feeling good about himself because of his cowardly denial, still stayed in Christ's company. Christ responded to Peter's trust by entrusting Peter with the community of the church.

When they had eaten their meal, Jesus said to Simon Peter, "Simon, son of John, do you love me more than these?" "Yes, Lord," he said, "you know that I love you." At which Jesus said, "Feed my lambs."

A second time he put his question, "Simon, son of John, do you love me?" "Yes, Lord," Peter said, "you know that I love you." Jesus replied, "Tend my sheep."

A third time Jesus asked him, "Simon, son of John, do you love me?" Peter was hurt because he had asked a third time, "Do you love me?" So he said to him: "Lord, you know everything. You know well that I love you." Jesus said to him, "Feed my sheep."

...When Jesus had finished speaking he said to him, "Follow me." (John 21:15-17, 19)

Sit erect. Imagine your heart as your center. Let yourself be aware of Christ there, present to you. Let this Scripture scene be played out in this place within you. Take Peter's part; note his feelings and his attitude about himself. Then, replay the scene with yourself as the lead character and recall what you dislike about yourself (see Recording above) as the background for your encounter with Jesus. Let Jesus question you. Respond, and then let him affirm you. End as you wish. Write a sentence or two to help you remember this Prayer Time.

Remembering

Take an off-moment to recall your friendship with the Lord. Ask yourself this question: What difference does one friendship make for me?

Prayer Time 7

Prayer: A Duty or a Privilege?

Relating

Ten minutes of prayer a day, especially if the day is heavily scheduled, can become a burden. One more activity! The reflective time each day can, however, be the one activity that will make sense of all the others in the day. Time for prayer can enrich everything else.

Thomas Merton, a convert from atheism, a monk and one of the most respected spiritual writers of our time, likened prayer to a beautiful sight he saw while traveling in Mexico. He stopped off in a small village and, in the warm mid-afternoon, he noticed two elderly Indian men walking slowly down the street, arms around each other. They were linked together and leaning on each other; obviously they were long-standing friends who were comfortable together. Talking at times and just walking at times, they "fit" together.

Two elderly Indians easily found time for each other because they had grown in friendship together. Prayer time is time for building a relationship. It takes time to "fit" together. In the beginning we may begrudge the time and effort given to daily communication with God. Yet, if we stay with the effort, our lives will change because of this relationship.

Reflecting and Recording

Try to recall—from this last week or from any part of your past—a time when you experienced God being with you. Write a few sentences recalling this.

Does prayer ever seem to be a duty to you? Did it seem a duty during this last week? If so, did you persevere anyway? What was the result?

Responding

Sit erect. Put yourself into the Lord's presence. You may use the centering exercise from Prayer Time 4 or the breathing exercise from Prayer Time 1. Closing your eyes may help. After you are present to the moment, read slowly Psalm 23. Like all of Scripture, Psalm 23 is God's Word.

The LORD is my shepherd; I shall not want.
In verdant pastures he gives me repose;
Beside restful waters he leads me;
he refreshes my soul.
He guides me in right paths
for his name's sake.

Even though I walk in the dark valley
I fear no evil; for you are at my side
With your rod and your staff
that give me courage.
You spread the table before me
in the sight of my foes;
You anoint my head with oil;
my cup overflows.
Only goodness and kindness follow me
all the days of my life;
And I shall dwell in the house of the LORD
for years to come.

Close your eyes again and stay with any image or word that keeps your attention. If time allows, go to a second image. Close by praying aloud the words of this psalm. Repeat the words slowly. Let yourself hear the words. Close by writing a reaction if you wish.

Remembering

Identify three occasions in the coming 24 hours when you will take a few moments to become aware of God's presence. A sentence or so of Psalm 23 may help you focus on God's presence in these moments.

27

Listening to God

Together: For the Session

Purpose

To listen to God in all the events of life
To understand how group sharing is supportive of faith life

Activity Sheets

16. Finding God in Everyday Life
17. Desert Experiences
18. Small-Group Sharing

See Facilitator's Notes, pp. 93-95

Alone: Until Next Session

Prayer Times

1. Noticing
2. Seeing in a Different Way
3. Living Another Day
4. The Real Thing
5. People
6. Getting a Good Look at Everything
7. Giving Thanks

Activity Sheet 16

Finding God in Everyday Life

1. Check any item which names a place where you have found God. Add any that are not mentioned.

☐ nature	☐ reading	☐ crisis times	☐ _____
☐ Bible	☐ recreation	☐ friendship	☐ _____
☐ sports	☐ challenges	☐ people	☐ _____
☐ music	☐ aloneness	☐ church	☐ _____
☐ sin	☐ conversion	☐ suffering	☐ _____
☐ study	☐ work	☐ family	☐ _____
☐ dreams	☐ confession	☐ celebrations	☐ _____
☐ everyday routine	☐ works of charity	☐ Holy Communion	☐ _____

2. List some places and events where you do *not* usually look for God. Then choose two of these and consider what God might be trying to say to you in them.

3. Has any event or circumstance in your life jolted you into listening to God's voice or searching for God's presence? Explain.

Activity Sheet 17

Desert Experiences

Living in a desert would change our attitudes toward life. Desert living demands getting down to the essentials of staying alive. Rich foods and drinks have to go; desert travelers survive on water and simple food—or they don't survive at all. Being overweight is dangerous. Each person must drop to a maintenance weight and calorie intake. Clothes? No room for fancy gowns or suits; only simple, sturdy protection from the burning sun and the nighttime cold.

All activity in the desert has to be slow—or else living things collapse from exertion. Energy is reserved for the essentials that maintain life. Little pleasures are the only pleasures. Little things, therefore, count a lot: a handful of dates, a drink of water, a spot of shade.

Getting one's bearings is everything—because getting lost means death. Everything in the desert looks alike at first. But soon one can appreciate how different two rocks are, or two scrub trees, or two hills. What would pass unnoticed in another place or time gets noticed and noted in the desert. Little differences are appreciated.

One little place or oasis can't support life for long. So most people who live in the desert are nomads, people on the move. They move to survive. Moving on—*slowly*—is a way of life.

The desert is a lonely place. There is little noise to distract one from thought. Although too much desert silence could be dangerous, a certain amount of it can call us to face what is important in our lives. Desert silence provides time to listen to life and to ourselves. The desert calls us to speak only about what counts.

A *desert attitude* can prepare us for prayer. Sometimes we may be given a desert experience through a loss that leaves us empty enough to listen. Sometimes a desert experience is thrust upon us by illness, giving us time for nothing but listening. Or we can create a desert experience by *making* time to reflect in a busy and sometimes crazy world.

The desert experience gives an opportunity to listen to God. To listen to another is to forget self, to notice the other person. To listen means to be open, to let go of my thoughts for the moment, to give up for a while on what I want to say.

To hear God we must regularly make a little silence. In that silence, I can hear the thousand ways God speaks to me each day in everything and everybody. Without some desert time alone with God, I may miss many of God's messages in my life.

1. If you have had any desert experiences in your life, name them.

2. How did each desert experience help you (or hinder you) from hearing God better in your life?

3. What qualities of the desert do you personally need so that you may hear God better in your life?

4. How can you give yourself what you need?

Activity Sheet 18

Small-Group Sharing

Small groups exist for many purposes. Some people can remain faithful to a diet only because they must face a Weight Watcher's group each week. Alcoholics Anonymous groups make sobriety possible for many people by supporting their efforts to stay away from alcohol. There are personal and marriage therapy groups, drug and sex addiction groups, and divorce recovery groups to name a few more. These groups help people because each person can stay in touch with others who care, others who will ask about failures and successes.

Groups, like those for parents who have lost a child, can give people support for a while until they get through a crisis. Other small groups, like the Japanese and Swedish quality-circle groups for automobile assembly, are task-oriented but value people knowing and respecting each other in order to do the work better. Still other small groups keep individuals believing and "fired up" with an ideal or a philosophy of life. The Communist Party, built on members meeting regularly in cells or small gatherings, is an example of the latter.

Small groups make a difference for the individual because other people in the group share his or her goals. Group members know each other and each person has a sense of belonging. Individual effort is made easier in a group and people who belong to one "get lost" less often.

Maybe it's time for us, the church, to learn from all this.

Prayer Time 1

Noticing

Relating

Every summer the Detroit River is the scene of the Midwest's hydroplane race. A hydroplane is a small, wide, rather flat-bottomed boat with a high-powered engine. The craft travels at high speeds and planes on top of the water, never really cutting into the river.

Our society encourages us to live like hydroplanes. We move quickly with many activities. Technology solves problems but does not lead us to ask the basic questions about what makes life worth living. Consequently, people live on the surface of life without thinking about what their experiences mean or about what is important. Many people no longer even know what they are feeling as they go through the day. We, like the hydroplanes, skim our way over the surface of life.

But our world and our lives express God and present God to us in a real way; they are sacramental. This is traditional, time-honored, basic Catholic teaching. Therefore, when we don't notice our everyday world and our everyday life, we miss God!

We have lost what we had as children—the ability to become spellbound by the things and people around us. To find God in creation we must experience it—touch, taste, smell, focus on it, listen intently. *Not* analyze it, own it, waste it. We must take note of it.

Reflecting and Recording

How would you assess—on a scale of 1 to 10—your own awareness of the everyday creation around you (1 = least aware; 10 = most aware)?

If you know any small children well enough to observe their interest and fascination with things around them, comment on those qualities.

Responding

Now the earth was a formless void.
There was darkness over the deep,
And God's spirit hovered over the water.

(Genesis 1:2, JB)

Relax, but sit erect. Do the breathing exercise until you are present to the moment and conscious of God's spirit throughout your being, especially in your center. Give this time.

Read the Scripture passage again. Relate that hovering spirit to the world you will experience as you go through your day—the light outside, the view from your window, the scene in your yard, the sky and so on. Connect the creative power of God to each bit of the created world you will pass through today.

Remembering

List the aspects of your life where you choose to take time to notice the "spirit hovering" today:

Prayer Time 2

Seeing in a Different Way

Relating

Norman had been homebound for many months with a painful bone cancer that he knew would take his life. He had been an active and responsible man. His disease now kept him housebound during a long, severe winter.

One day the dreary, late winter warmed just enough for his wife to take him on a short ride to the neighborhood shopping plaza. He waited in the car for 10 minutes as she did some quick errands. In that 10 minutes Norman took note of how the sunshine occasionally broke through, the way people walked, how parents dragged their children, the expressions on faces, the interplay of people. He spoke of that 10 minutes for days. Of course he had visited that shopping plaza scores of times when he had been healthy. The parking lot had not changed; he had.

The discipline—and discipline it is—of appreciating ordinary events and people can help us see life in a new way. Noticing ordinary things takes deliberate effort for most of us. Major happenings like birth, job loss, moving, promotion, death or financial loss force themselves upon our consciousness. The ordinary realities of life simply go by—or we go by them:

> There were bells, on the hill
> but I never heard them ringing....
> There were birds in the sky
> but I never saw them winging....
> (Meredith Wilson, *The Music Man*)

Helen Keller had eyes that were blind and ears deaf from birth, but she has helped countless people see and hear in a different way. Helen Keller's words: "The best and most beautiful things in the world cannot be seen or even touched. They must be felt with the heart."

We can listen to our everyday world speak to us in two ways: (1) in the actual event, object or person; (2) in the reactions stirred up within us. How I am affected and how I feel is as important as the reality itself.

Reflecting and Recording

In the past 24 hours of my life, how was I affected by each encounter with a place, a part of creation, an event, a person? (Just note your reactions in as much detail as your time allows with no judgments about whether or not you should feel this way.)

Responding

> This is the day the LORD has made;
> let us be glad and rejoice in it. (Psalm 118:24)

Sit erect, relaxed but alert. Take a few moments to become present to this moment. Put yourself in God's presence. Express whatever you feel about your experiences of the past 24 hours.

Remembering

Plan several times "in between" appointments, chores or classes to note your emotional reactions to situations, persons, or the things you see. Try to make an act of trust that God is somehow communicating to you in them. List these "in-between" times now:

Prayer Time 3

Living Another Day

Relating

The world—and what goes on in it—is not like a house or place I live in. It is not separate from me. The world—and my little piece of the world—expresses God. It expresses me, too. The same God made both the world and me, and God communicates through both.

God created this world deliberately. God had his Son in mind as he shaped the world and us. The love he has for that Son is expressed in both us and creation.

> He [the Son] is the image of the invisible God, the firstborn of all creatures. In him, everything in heaven and on earth was created, things visible and invisible...; all were created through him, and for him. (Colossians 1:15-16)

We can make any single day of our lives the subject of our prayer. Here is one way of "praying" a day: First, begin with the conviction that God is in your day and is communicating with you. Next, take time to notice events/objects/persons and their effect on you. Finally, ask: What is God saying to me in this person, this event, this struggle, this joy? What am I feeling about this now?

If we continue this kind of reflective discernment, we will begin to see God in situations even as they are unfolding.

Reflecting and Recording

Since I prayed yesterday, these are the places, happenings and people I have encountered:

Responding

> Where can I go from your spirit?
> from your presence where can I flee?
>
> (Psalm 139:7)

Pray your day using the steps as described above.

Relax while sitting erect. Place your list from Reflect and Record in your memory and in your heart. Concentrate on your heart. Center yourself there. Take time for this. Accept, and become aware of, God's presence within you. Accept his loving you and his nearness.

In God's presence go over your list of experiences and note their effect on you. If one particular experience seems important, stay with that one.

Ask: What was my reaction as the event took place? What is my reaction now? How is this experience of a particular person, place or thing calling me to a stronger friendship with God? If not, why?

Remembering

Write one resolution to help you be more open to God through the experiences of the next 24 hours:

Prayer Time 4

The Real Thing

Relating

> Earth's crammed with heaven
> And every common bush afire with God;
> And only he who sees takes off his shoes—
> The rest sit round it and pluck blackberries.
> (Elizabeth Barrett Browning, "For Those Who See")

While Moses was tending sheep and goats, he heard God's voice come from a burning bush. God told Moses to take off his shoes because the ground was holy; God was present.

Since God is present, moment by moment, we could walk barefoot all day. Reverence for life is a necessary attitude for hearing God. Having reverence requires discipline, however, since life is so easily devalued in our society.

We must begin by reverencing our own lives, seeing "the holy" in the way our lives really are. We must reverence the larger world, too—the way this world really is. There is no perfect marriage, no perfectly integrated personality, no perfect world! Our act of faith, of reverence, is in this flawed and sinful world, not some ideal one. God communicates through our imperfect reality since imperfect reality is all we have.

Our attitude of reverence can be destroyed if we live with regrets, focus more on what is missing than what is present, or keep wishing "if only"—if only my parents had been different, if only my job were better, if only I had both legs, if only my children had turned out better. That world does not exist.

Another enemy of reverence for our present reality

can be a distorted sense of religion. Certain types of people are sometimes seen as religious models. The so-called "real" believer is thought to be always in control, always smiling, never upset, unattached to worldly pleasures of any kind, seldom struggling with temptation. Unfortunately, many people judge themselves to be nonreligious because they do not fit that plastic idea of holiness.

God speaks through the real world. He—or she—is there in our struggles, our failures and our successes. Don't limit God by deciding beforehand what is religious and what is not. Give God a better chance of being heard by "taking off your shoes" as you walk through this day.

Reflecting and Recording

I find God most easily in these situations:

These are the the parts of my life where I am least inclined to look for God's presence today:

Responding

...I call you friends,
since I have made known to you all that I heard
from my Father.
It was not you who chose me,
it was I who chose you....(John 15:15-16)

Choose a centering or breathing exercise to help you become present to this moment and aware of God's presence. Repeat the last two lines of the Scripture quotation over and over. Hear Christ say those words to you. Let your mind stay with those words.

If time allows, look ahead to a situation in the coming day that does not easily speak to you of God. What might

God be saying to you in this situation? Ask him. Write a response if you can.

Remembering

Choose a person, event or experience in which you would have been unlikely to notice God in the past. Look for God's presence there now.

Prayer Time 5

People

Relating

The human person is the best of all God's creation. God made us in his own image and likeness. Noticing people, going beneath the surface, is essential for listening to God.

We need to begin with the people God places close to us—like family and intimate friends. Eventually, we can also look at the people we just brush up against throughout the day.

Despite our external differences in education, physical features, kinds of jobs, types of clothing or cars, we human beings are basically alike. We must not be stopped by outward appearances. We are much more alike than we seem.

We all:

• look to be loved for ourselves and not simply for accomplishments
• have an inward desire to love another, even though we may be out of practice
• are unsure and afraid at times
• want peace and a place to call home
• feel the same variety of emotions
• are sometimes lonely
• have a long history of many influences on the way we act
• have to struggle.

Despite our sameness, we still do not easily let others get to know us. Most of our lives are spent without anyone caring much about our "real" inner self. In western society a person is often a number, a job, a car on the expressway, a face in a crowd. It takes a little noticing to see and appreciate an individual human being.

Each human person reflects God by being human, not superhuman. Our most solid Catholic teaching is that God has become fully human and remains human forever in Jesus Christ. He didn't just look human or go through the motions. The Son of God is fully God and fully a human being. His humanity (and ours) reveals God.

In the play *The Rainmaker*, Lizzie looks at her plain, middle-aged father playing cards. She is doing dishes in the kitchen. At first she only sees the same everyday man she always has seen. But as she keeps looking she begins to notice more. Here's how she describes the process:

> I'll see little things I never saw in him before. Good things and bad things—queer little habits I never noticed he had—and ways of talking I never paid any mind to. And suddenly I knew who he is—and I love him so much I could cry! And I want to thank God I took the time to see him real.
> (Richard Nash, *The Rainmaker*)

Reflecting and Recording

Who did I meet as I went through the past 24 hours?

As I replay each encounter, what emotions do I notice in myself? How did each of the encounters affect me?

Responding

Then God said: "Let us make man in our image, after our likeness." (Genesis 1:26)

Sit erect. Center yourself. Concentrate on yourself right here, right now. Close your eyes for a few minutes and let God choose you. Notice how aware he is of you.

Choose any person you met in the past 24 hours and pay close attention to that person now. Does that person in any way reveal some aspect of God to you? Something about yourself?

Write a few phrases about noticing God in people.

Remembering

List three people you will meet in the coming 24 hours. What will be your approach to each?

Prayer Time 6

Getting a Good Look at Everything

Relating

God is to be found in our real world. Part of reality is facing death. Death is a fact of life.

> Man's days are like those of grass;
>   like a flower of the field he blooms;
> The wind sweeps over him and he is gone,
>   and his place knows him no more.
> (Psalm 103:15-16)

Facing one's own death is central to a life of faith. How we face death determines how we face life. If we ignore or deny the reality of death by constant activity, then we will cling to life desperately. A clinging person is never free.

Facing death may not be comfortable but, in doing so, we are facing reality and, hence, giving God another avenue of communication with us.

Reflecting and Recording

If today were the last day I had to live, I would make sure to do the following:

If I could pick one person to say good-bye to, who would it be? What two lines would I say?

Responding

> Teach us to number our days aright,
>   that we may gain wisdom of heart.
> (Psalm 90:12)

Relax. Sit upright. Let each part of your body relax. Feel the tension slowly leaving the soles of your feet. Work your way up your entire body, releasing tension. Then let your body be supported in God's hands. Feel yourself resting solidly on God. Stay with that for a while.

Mentally go through your coming day and look at each person, event and place as if this were the last day of your life. Spend as much time as you can. Ask the Lord to help you with your responses.

Remembering

Use this hypothetical "if" ("if this were my last day") to look differently at everything that comes your way today. Choose one thing or one person you will especially notice with this in mind:

Prayer Time 7

Giving Thanks

Relating

> "Dedicate yourselves to thankfulness."
> (Colossians 3:15)

Most of us are not particularly good at being grateful. As we struggle with life, we can forget that life is also a gift. We can easily be more aware of what is missing in our lives than of what is present for us. Developing a grateful heart takes deliberate, daily practice.

Facing death is a solid path to appreciating the gifts of a lifetime or a day—gifts that are easily taken for granted. The following excerpt from one dying man's last will and testament bespeaks such gratitude:

Therefore, in the presence of death, of the total and definitive separation from the present life, I deem it my duty to exalt the gift, the good fortune, the beauty, the destiny of this same fleeting existence: Lord, I thank you for having called me into life, and even more so, making me a Christian, for having regenerated and destined me to the fullness of life.

Likewise, I feel obliged to thank and to bless those who were the means of conveying to me the gifts of life...: my parents, those who educated me, loved me, did good to me, helped me, surrounded me with good example, with care, affection, trust, goodness, kindness, friendship....I look with gratitude on the natural and spiritual relationships which have given origin, assistance, support, significance to my humble existence; how many gifts, how many beautiful and noble things, how much hope have I received in this world!....

I close my eyes on this sorrowful, dramatic and magnificent world, invoking once again on her behalf the divine goodness. (Excerpt from "Last Will of Pope Paul VI," *Origins*, August 31, 1978)

Death is an ending. Facing endings can teach us gratitude.

Reflecting, Recording and Responding

Begin with the relaxation exercise from the last Prayer Time. Then go over your day—the events, appointments, people encountered. Try to see each as a gift from God—a personal gift to you. Give thanks to God for each in your own words.

I am thankful today for the following:

What/whom do I take for granted?

For what/whom do I find it most difficult to be grateful?

Remembering

I will give thanks to you, O LORD,
with all my heart. (Psalm 9:2)

Decide how you will deliberately show gratitude today:

'Centering' and the Presence of God

Together: For the Session

Purpose

To begin to learn centering prayer
To develop a keener awareness of the presence of God

Activity Sheet

19. Centering

See Facilitator's Notes, pp. 95-97

Alone: Until Next Session

Prayer Times

1. The Our Father
2. 'Our Father in Heaven'
3. 'Hallowed Be Your Name!'
4. 'Your Kingdom Come, Your Will Be Done...'
5. 'Give Us Today Our Daily Bread'
6. 'Forgive Us...'
7. '...As We Forgive'

Activity Sheet 19

Centering

When we come to a halt in our busyness and try to think or pray, our minds usually continue to jump from one thought to another. Our insides continue to race. Centering is a way of getting ourselves to let go of everything and to become aware of the present moment. It is a means of relaxing our bodies and slowing down our minds. Centering helps us to quiet down and become present to ourselves.

Any one of many simple techniques help us to relax and center. Choose the ones that are personally helpful—or discover or invent your own.

In the Prayer Times several centering techniques are used:

• breathing slowly and consciously

• listening to one's name repeated over and over

• relaxing the body, part by part, from the soles of the feet to the top of the head

• feeling the support of the chair on one's body and relaxing against that support

Not mentioned are two other helpful methods:

• paying attention to one's own heartbeat (which was tried in last Session's prayer) or consciously listening to the rhythm of a clock. (Then become aware of God deliberately giving you another moment of life with each count. Remember that God is here for you now.)

• concentrating on a simple object such as the flame of a candle, a flower, a cross, a rock. (Then imagine God looking as gently and deliberately at you.)

The centering method is not important. What does matter is that you learn to slow down your thoughts and feelings in order to give attention to God and God's communication.

Prayer Time 1
The Our Father

Relating

"Lord, teach us to pray...." (Luke 11:1)

Jesus answered this request with the Our Father which is the prayer form that all Christians agree upon. It is meant to be used as a model or pattern for prayer, not a rote prayer. Some also consider it a direction for the process of prayer—a road map for the journey. The Our Father's importance isn't so much in its particular words as in its formula: Address God as a living parent, praise his name, pray for the coming of his Kingdom and so on.

In the next nine Prayer Times we will center on the Our Father, taking one phrase at a time. We will deepen our understanding by seeing how it fits into our lives and the lives of the community.

The New Testament gives us two translations of the Lord's Prayer. We will use the one in Matthew's Gospel as our text:

> Our Father in heaven,
> hallowed be your name,
> your kingdom come,
> your will be done
> on earth as it is in heaven.
> Give us today our daily bread,
> and forgive us the wrong we have done
> as we forgive those who wrong us.
> Subject us not to the trial
> but deliver us from the evil one. (Matthew 6:9-14)

The authors of both the Old and New Testaments see God as having an abiding, personal relationship with us. As Father, God is the source of life, everyone's life! We share in this life as children share the life of their parents. Jesus addressed God in very familiar terms: In Gethsemane he called God *Abba*, or Daddy. He talked of God's love being greater than that of a human mother. Jesus' parable of the Prodigal Son is also a parable of the Loving Father. God, for Jesus and for us, has all the attributes of a loving parent. The power to whom we pray is personal, intimate and caring.

> Yet, O LORD, you are our father;
> we are the clay and you the potter:
> we are all the work of your hands.
> (Isaiah 64:7)

Reflecting and Recording

Name some characteristics of a perfect, loving parent—father or mother.

If God is the Father of us all, what relationship does this imply between me and people of other races, religions, nations?

As I use the word *our* before Father, can I consciously include in my thoughts the members of my small group, my parish, the worldwide Church, the entire human family as praying *with* me? Are there any obstacles to my being at one with these people as I pray?

Responding

Relax and breathe deeply. Clear your mind as best you can. Let your Father love you as his special creation! After some time of quiet, tell your Parent how grateful you are to be his creation.

Remembering

Try to see all the people in your life today as part of the "our" in the first phrase of the Lord's Prayer. Pray "Our Father" often as you go through your day.

Prayer Time 2

'Our Father in Heaven'

Relating

What is heaven? Is it fluffy clouds and blue skies? Is it a faraway place? Are there gates and harps? Is it complete peace?

Where is heaven? Is it up? Is it experienced only when we die?

We've all heard statements like this one by Robert Browning: "God's in his heaven—All's right with the world." Or we talk about "the man upstairs" or "pie in the sky when we die." This kind of God and this kind of heaven seem once-removed from our here-and-now lives.

But Jesus spent his life telling us that both God and heaven are very near. Heaven is wherever God is; and in Jesus, God is *with us* at all times and in all places.

> They were to seek God, yes to grope for him and perhaps eventually to find him—though he is not really far from any one of us. "In him we live and move and have our being...." (Acts 17:27-28)

Reflecting and Recording

How do I respond to the fact that God is always with me? That I am with God now?

Does this reality affect my life in any way? If so, how?

Responding

Close your eyes; breathe deeply and relax. Let your experience of God's presence become more of a reality. Listen to your Father. Enjoy the God—and the heaven—within you.

Remembering

As you go about your work, remind yourself often that "In him we live and move and have our being...." (Acts 17:28). Repeat this verse throughout the day.

Prayer Time 3

'Hallowed Be Your Name!'

Relating

In Scripture a name says who and what a person is. When God communicates his name, he communicates who he is. God's name in the Old Testament is *I Am* or *The One Who Is*.

This name inspires a sense of awe and reverence—an interesting counterpoint to *Abba*. We know God as a loving Father, but we must also be aware of this more-than-words-can-describe aspect of God: the feeling we get when we see a beautiful sunset or sunrise. We can be in awe of God in his many works of nature—mountains, oceans, canyons.

In intimacy yet reverence, closeness yet otherness, God—and his name—are holy, hallowed. We pray that we too may become holy (whole) by hallowing his name.

Reflecting and Recording

I use these names when I address God:

My favorite name for God is

Why?

In what ways am I aware of both the intimate and the awe-inspiring God?

Responding

Relax and breathe deeply; calm your mind. Use the name for God with which you are most comfortable. Address God by this name; be silent awhile. Again speak this name; again be silent. Continue to relax in saying your God's name with love.

Remembering

Frequently address God by your favorite name today. Write it, read it, sing it, say it—do whatever helps you hallow his name.

petitions. We are asking the Father to establish his rule, his will, everywhere "on earth as it is in heaven."

Jesus compared the Reign of God to a pearl of great price or a treasure hidden in a field (Matthew 13:44-46). The full establishment of this Kingdom was the vision and mission of the early Church. And it is our vision and mission too.

Praying for the Reign of God on earth can be both exciting and frightening. The earth is, after all, *us*. Are *we* willing to be changed for the sake of this Reign?

Reflecting and Recording

What needs to be changed in the Church and society so that the Kingdom of God can come and God's will can be done in us?

What changes do I need to make so that the Kingdom can be realized in me?

Prayer Time 4

'Your Kingdom Come, Your Will Be Done...'

Relating

To pray for the coming of God's Kingdom—or Rule or Reign—and to ask that the will of God be done, are other-directed and, in some ways, future-oriented

What am I willing to do right now to begin the process?

Acknowledging my reliance on God does not mean that I do nothing. Quite the contrary: I use my talents, skills and abilities with even more dedication to give back to the Father and to share with others what he has so generously given me.

When we seriously accept our very lives as God's gift, we open ourselves up to receive even more of God's goodness.

Reflecting and Recording

Jesus taught us to ask daily for what we need. To do this, we must be aware of our real needs.

What are my physical and material needs at this time?

Responding

Relax and breathe deeply. Present to your Father your answers to the last two questions. Be quiet awhile, knowing that your Father is responding.

Remembering

Write in your appointment book, or in some other visible place, one thing you are doing this day to let God's Kingdom come.

What are my spiritual and emotional needs?

Prayer Time 5

'Give Us Today Our Daily Bread'

What are the needs of my family, my community, my world?

Relating

In asking our Father for our daily bread, we are asking for more than just food. We are petitioning for *all* the basic needs of life.

Whenever we ask for something from anyone—a friend, a parent, God—we acknowledge that we are not self-sufficient. That is why asking is so difficult for some of us to do. We would rather go without than be indebted to someone else.

But asking for "bread" characterizes us as Christians. By requesting that God fill our basic life needs, we are honestly saying: *I am dependent on God for my life!*

How will I give back to the Father and to my community the "bread" already given to me this day?

Responding

Relax and breathe deeply. Remember, you are in contact with God who loves you and wants to satisfy your daily needs. Be quiet and listen. Then thank him for all he has already given you.

Remembering

With each meal or snack today, remember how your Father has filled your needs in the past and is filling your needs today. Trust him to provide you with "bread" tomorrow.

The opening focus of the Our Father is on God—his name, his Kingdom and his will for us. Then the focus shifts to us and our personal needs as we pray for bread, the very sustenance of life. In our very asking we affirm our belief that we are dependent on God for everything.

Next we pray for forgiveness. "Sins," "trespasses," "debts," "wrongs"—various translations of the Our Father use different words to express our deep sense of "missing the mark," violating others' rights, owing more than we can repay, breaking God's law.

Whatever word we use, however, we know we stand in need of God's healing forgiveness. And God's forgiveness is *always* there for us. But we need to open ourselves to *receive* this forgiveness over and over again.

We pray today to receive the forgiveness of God. Only then can we pass that forgiveness on.

Reflecting and Recording

God's forgiveness is his gift to us. We need to accept this gift and forgive ourselves.

Right now I most need God to forgive me for these sins, trespasses and debts:

Prayer Time 6

'Forgive Us...'

Relating

Pray, slowly and thoughtfully, the prayer Jesus taught us.

Our Father in heaven,
hallowed be your name,
your kingdom come,
your will be done
on earth as it is in heaven.
Give us today our daily bread,
and forgive us the wrong we have done
as we forgive those who wrong us.
Subject us not to the trial
but deliver us from the evil one. (Matthew 6:9-14)

Right now I most need to forgive myself for the following sins, trespasses or debts:

Perhaps the following prayer might help.

Responding

Relax and breathe deeply. As you do so, let God's unconditional love and forgiveness flow through you. Let God love you and forgive you. Conclude with this prayer:

My Father, I need your forgiveness.
I accept it today and I also forgive myself.
Help me to accept myself as you accept me
    throughout the day.

Remembering

When you are tempted to start putting yourself down or belittling yourself today, say, "My Father forgives me; I forgive me, too!"

Prayer Time 7

'... As We Forgive'

Relating

Only one petition of the Our Father includes a condition: "Forgive us...*as we forgive*."

Often we hold others responsible for the hurts and wrongs in our lives. And at times they are. People do cause us pain. People have ignored us, stepped on us, used us, abandoned us, forgotten us. These are real hurts. Social systems, government bureaucracy and even the church have caused some of us untold anxiety and pain.

We are not asked to pretend that unjust and painful events didn't happen or that we aren't affected by the sins of those who have wronged us. But we are asked to forgive, to absolve, to release from debt. *Webster's New Collegiate Dictionary* defines *forgive* as "to give up resentment or claim to requital on account of an offense."

Just as our Father forgives us even before we ask, we, in turn, must release others from their debts to us. We must absolve them. We must let go and surrender the hurt, the pain and, especially, the sense of power that bearing a grudge can give us.

And we must do this over and over again. Forgiveness is a daily discipline. Only by releasing and forgiving others will we be able to grow. Only by passing on our Father's forgiveness to others will we ourselves be healed.

Reflecting and Recording

This exercise requires time, thought and, at least, your desire to forgive.

List all those who have hurt you in any way. You may want to go back to your childhood, your teen years and so on.

When you are finished, go back and recall the hurt associated with each name. Then let it go! Forgive that person. You might say something like:

Through the forgiveness Christ has given me, I forgive and release N. _____.

You may wish to continue this exercise over a period of several days or weeks.

Responding

Relax and note any new sense of freedom you may now feel. Thank your Father for giving you his great gift of forgiveness. And ask for the power of the Spirit so that *you* can continue to forgive.

Remembering

At day's end, look back and focus on any people that you need to forgive. With the power of the forgiving Christ within you, let go of the hurt and forgive each person. And don't forget to forgive yourself too! (You may wish to make this a nightly practice.)

Difficulties in Praying

Together: For the Session

Purpose

To note some difficulties in prayer
To learn how to work through the difficulties

Activity Sheet

20. Dealing With Dry Times

See Facilitator's Notes, pp. 97-99

Alone: Until Next Session

Prayer Times

1. Deliverance From Evil
2. Praising God
3. Asking God
4. Asking for Specifics
5. Asking Again and Again
6. Praying for Another
7. Pray for Me!

Activity Sheet 20

Dealing With 'Dry' Times

Most people experience some dryness in prayer.

We begin our prayer journey "strong," enjoying our time of prayer. After a while, however, we may discover that the "honeymoon is over." It may be a week, a month or a year before dryness comes, but it usually does.

Dry describes the way we feel when the good feelings are gone: God doesn't seem to be with us anymore. We may even question whether he ever was.

A dry time can be a time of growth; it can be a special time of grace. It gives us an opportunity to choose prayer as a way of choosing God. Good feelings and self-satisfaction are no longer the reason to make time for prayer; instead, we continue to pray simply as a choice for God. This can be good purification of our love for God.

No relationship is built on highs and constant good feelings. Spouses, family members, friends have to be there for each other, to make time for each other, even when doing so feels like work or a task.

No human being is always up. Going through mood swings is normal.

We are called to deepen our relationships with God—not to have more satisfying feelings. Yet our temptation in times of dryness is to stop praying or to shorten our prayer times. We must resist the temptation. We need to stay faithful to the time we make to be with the Lord. Being steady—that is what friendship is all about.

Consider which of the following causes of dryness may be yours:

1. being physically indisposed, nervous or tense

2. suffering from deeply hurt feelings

3. being emotionally upset or anxious about such things as job, health, children or love

4. in a dry period—one of those down times in the ups-and-downs that are part of everything in life

5. in need of an atmosphere of quiet or a place conducive to prayer

6. unable to unwind or "get into" the presence of God

7. in need of more time, more motivation or more appreciation for prayer

8. not yet comfortable with any method of praying

9. feeling bad about one's self and, therefore, withdrawing from God and others

10. having doubts about faith

11. feeling distant from God because of a constant temptation or sin (an overwhelming ambition or a compulsive desire for money, a person, a thing, a position)

12. feeling overburdened by high ideals, by trying too hard, by becoming discouraged at a seeming lack of progress

13. not "listening" enough

Prayer Time 1

Deliverance From Evil

Relating

> Subject us not to the trial
> but deliver us from the evil one.

The Lord's Prayer comes to an abrupt conclusion with these words. We request that God not allow us to fall victim to temptation, that trials, suffering and death not overwhelm us. In other words, we ask the Father not to let us be tempted beyond our strength.

Jesus was tempted in the desert (Matthew 4:1-11). But by affirming his total dedication to his Father, Jesus triumphed and was delivered. Jesus was also tested in Gethsemani (Matthew 26:36-46). But again he was delivered by his Father—our Father.

Each day we also are presented with trials. Do we, like Jesus, rely on our Father and his power working in us? Do we call on our Father for strength? Or do we try to go it alone, fall on our face and then, only as a last resort, "try God"?

The Lord's Prayer, prayed regularly, can help us little by little to change our hearts. It helps us learn to love, surrender and depend on God for all that we need. It prompts us to ask God's help to handle the very real evil we experience in a responsible, Christ-like way.

Jesus Christ, who lives within us, is our deliverer. He is God's answer to our prayer: "Lead us not into temptation, but deliver us from evil."

Reflecting and Recording

In what ways have I been "delivered" in the past?

What real difference will it make in my day-to-day life if I pattern my life more consciously on the Lord's Prayer?

What can I resolve to do right now to begin this patterning?

Responding

Breathe deeply and relax. Let the Father assure you that he will continue to deliver you.

Remembering

Reread your resolutions above. What one thing will you do today? Remember throughout the day that God is with you!

Prayer Time 2

Praising God

Relating

> For thine is the kingdom,
> the power and the glory
> forever and forever.

This doxology, or praise of God, was added by the early church to the Lord's Prayer. It calls us to be aware of the great majesty and power of our Father and to respond by praising him through our actions and our words. To praise God is an act of love and reverence.

Reflecting and Recording

I find it difficult to praise God because...

I find it easy to praise God because...

Responding

The Hebrews wrote beautiful psalms (songs) to praise God. Slowly read Psalm 8:

> O LORD, our Lord,
>   how glorious is your name over all the earth!
>   You have exalted your majesty above the heavens.
>
> Out of the mouths of babes and sucklings
>   you have fashioned praise because of your foes,
>   to silence the hostile and the vengeful.
>
> When I behold your heavens, the work of your fingers,
>   the moon and the stars which you set in place—
>
> What is man that you should be mindful of him,
>   or the son of man that you should care for him?
>
> You have made him little less than the angels,
>   and crowned him with glory and honor.
>
> You have given him rule over the works of your hands,
>   putting all things under his feet:
>
> All sheep and oxen,
>   yes, and the beasts of the field,
>
> The birds of the air, the fishes of the sea,
>   and whatever swims the paths of the seas.
>
> O LORD, Our Lord,
>   how glorious is your name over all the earth!

Remembering

Throughout the day take some moments to praise the Father. You may want to use one of the following prayers or one of your own choice: "For yours is the Kingdom." "O Lord, our Lord, how glorious is your name." "Give thanks to the Lord for he is good."

Prayer Time 3

Asking God

Relating

Prayer of petition is an act of trust that God has power in our lives and that God loves us so much that we can trust him with our needs. In prayer we put ourselves into our Father's hands, surrendering and opening ourselves up to receive his gifts.

If I never ask God for anything for myself, it *could* mean that I don't feel worthy of God's gifts, worthy of God's love. These feelings can pose a barrier to communication with God—and with anyone else.

Never asking God for anything for myself or for another could also mean I'm not willing to be vulnerable. If I don't ask, I can't get turned down or be disappointed.

Reflecting and Recording

What father among you will give his son a snake if he asks for a fish, or hand him a scorpion if he asks for an egg? If you, with all your sins, know how to give your children good things, how much more will the heavenly Father give the Holy Spirit to those who ask him. (Luke 11:11-13)

Write your personal reaction to these words of Jesus.

For what have you asked God in your life? (If you have not asked for anything, how would you explain this?)

Do you believe yourself worthy to receive what you ask for? Why or why not?

Responding

> If you with all your sins, know how to give your children good things, how much more will the heavenly Father give the Holy Spirit to those who ask him. (Luke 11:13)

Reread this sentence several times until you can say it from memory. Now relax, but sit upright. Breathe deeply. Become conscious of your breathing and pay attention to your breathing until you are centered.

Concentrate on God who is breathing breath and spirit into you. Receive God's own life. Accept it.

Keep repeating the phrase from Luke: "If you...." Savor the words and experience them as you say them.

Finally, ask your Father to give you his Holy Spirit. Tell him what you need the Spirit of God to do within you.

Remembering

At least once today, stop and consciously allow God's Spirit to work in some action of yours.

> The Spirit too helps us in our weakness, for we do not know how to pray as we ought; but the Spirit himself makes intercession for us with groanings that cannot be expressed in speech. He who searches hearts knows what the Spirit means, for the Spirit intercedes for the saints as God himself wills. (Romans 8:26-27)

Reflecting and Recording

Look over the prayer requests which you wrote in Prayer Time 3. Assess each request as to whether the petition is (a) clear and specific, (b) something you honestly want, (c) something the Holy Spirit praying in you would ask.

Write a clear and confident petition—or several of them—expressing what you most want to ask of the Lord at this time.

Prayer Time 4
Asking for Specifics

Relating

Failure to ask God for what we need can be a failure to trust God. We can miss who God is for us and not give God the opportunity to be a Father or Mother for us. We can deprive God of the chance to be like a parent—a role God desires.

Of course we don't want to be like the little child on Santa's lap, ticking off a list of trivial things that really don't matter. Doing so weakens an adult relationship with God. We should ask God for what really matters to us. And we need to ask God specifically and clearly. Praying in vague generalities is not good communication. We need to be real.

Recall Jesus' words: "How much more will the heavenly Father give the Holy Spirit to those who ask him" (Luke 11:13). The Holy Spirit is God's greatest gift because the Spirit is God sharing himself, actually giving himself. That Spirit gives us love and wisdom beyond our own. The Spirit will teach us how to be real with the Father and what we should ask for in prayer.

Ask yourself if these are consistent with what God wants for you.

Responding

> Ask and you shall receive; seek and you shall find; knock and it shall be opened to you. (Luke 11:9)

Take enough time to relax in God's presence. Hear God call your name with deliberate care and affection. Hear this over and over again.

Imagine Jesus saying the above words from Luke 11:9. Hear them being said to you over and over. Write down with boldness and confidence anything you now wish to ask for.

give them swift justice. But when the Son of Man comes, will he find any faith on the earth?"

(Luke 18:1-8)

This parable, like all parables, has *one* main point. The story does not tell us that God is like the corrupt judge or that we need to pester God to get a hearing; only this: We should persevere in prayer.

Many saints prayed for years and years for the same gift. Like the saints, we must also keep asking! To stop means taking the chance of forgetting who our Father is—and who we are.

Reflecting and Recording

If you can, name any petitions(s) for which you have persevered in prayer over a long period of time. What keeps you asking?

Remembering

Commit Luke 11:9 to memory so you can recall quietly Jesus' words throughout the day. Also notice how God may be answering your prayer.

Prayer Time 5

Asking Again and Again

Relating

To give up asking God for help may mean we are losing confidence in God or in ourselves. Or maybe we are beginning to lose sight of our dependence on God. The Holy Spirit praying in us will give us the power to persevere in our requests and to purify our trust in our Father.

If you have dropped some petitions over time, what are they? Why have you stopped asking for these?

> [Jesus] told them a parable on the necessity of praying always and not losing heart: "Once there was a judge in a certain city who respected neither God nor man. A widow in that city kept coming to him saying, 'Give me my rights against my opponent.' For a time he refused, but finally he thought, 'I care little for God nor man, but this widow is wearing me out. I am going to settle in her favor or she will end by doing me violence.'" The Lord said, "Listen to what the corrupt judge has to say. Will not God then do justice to his chosen who call out to him day and night? Will he delay long over them, do you suppose? I tell you, he will

Check over the requests you listed in Prayer Times 3 and 4. How have they been answered? Will you persevere in asking?

Responding

"Teacher," a man in the crowd replied, "I have brought my son to you because he is possessed by a mute spirit....If...you can do anything to help us, please do!" Jesus said, "'If you can?' Everything is possible to a man who trusts." The boy's father immediately exclaimed, "I do believe! Help my lack of trust!" (Mark 9:17, 22-24)

Sit erect. Center on Jesus' presence. Take time to picture yourself before him. Try to be aware of your feelings—and of any hesitancy or lack of trust. Looking at Jesus, pray the distraught father's prayer in the last line of the Scripture passage over and over.

Remembering

What do you request of God today? Resolve to bring this request to the Lord in a trusting and persevering way several times today.

Prayer Time 6

Praying for Another

Relating

We Catholics believe that *together* we are the Body of Christ in the world. Baptized into the Body of Christ, we believe that the good and the evil we do affects one another. We have a profound effect on each other even if

our actions are not known to anyone else. There is simply no way to be a private Catholic Christian. We are members of one body.

We each have spiritual energy within us. Prayer channels that energy through our one body—the Body of Christ. Whenever we think about another person and pray for him or her with love, our energy is concentrated on that person, and Jesus Christ touches, heals and opens that person. Together we are the body in which Jesus does this.

There is, therefore, great power in our prayers for another, power far greater than any of us has alone. That power is God's Spirit within us, the Body of Christ.

Being genuinely willing to intercede for someone also means being willing to give myself for the other, putting his or her welfare ahead of my own for a while. Real intercessory prayer thus involves more than a quick mention of someone's name to God. It means being willing to hear God's call to become an *answer to prayer* by doing something for the very person for whom we intercede.

Jesus interceded for others. Listen to this prayer for his disciples on the last evening of his life:

> For these [disciples] I pray—
> not for the world
> but for these you have given me,
> for they are really yours....
> I am in the world no more,
> but these are in the world
> as I come to you.
> O Father most holy,
> protect them with your name which you have given
>   me....
> I say all this while I am still in the world
> that they may share my joy completely....
> I do not ask you to take them out of the world,
> but to guard them from the evil one.
>
> (John 17:9-15)

Reflecting and Recording

Name the one or two persons for whom you have prayed with the most energy?

Did your prayer make a difference in the person or the situation? In you? Explain.

Bring into your presence and God's the person you are most concerned about. Concentrate on the person and his or her needs. Remember God's presence to you both. Offer that person to God—confidently. Ask God to take care of that person.

Remembering

During the "in-between" moments of your day, intercede for this same person. Is there any way that *you* might be an answer to prayer for that person?

Name a person you are deeply concerned about at present. Are you willing to intercede for this person with God? What might be demanded of you?

Prayer Time 7

Pray for Me!

Relating

Our Catholic belief in the Communion of Saints follows from our belief that all who are baptized form the Body of Christ. Even death does not separate us from the abiding influence we have on each other. We can pray for the deceased—and they can pray for us.

Being part of the Communion of Saints also means we can intercede for each other in this life. The Bible calls us, the people of the church, *saints*—not because we are perfect, but because God's Holy Spirit lives in us. God's life in us is a great power in our church community.

It is when we ask someone to pray for us that many of us independent and image-conscious moderns express our belief that the people of the church form Christ's body. The more specific our requests—the more we can actually name what we need in particular—the greater our trust in the community of the church.

Strangely, we often do not even ask the prayers of people with whom we share a spiritual and sacramental relationship—spouse, children, parents, godchildren.

On the last evening of his life Jesus interceded intensely for the disciples. He prayed from his heart. (See the passage quoted from John in Prayer Time 6). But then Jesus prays very deliberately *for us*. Have you ever thought of Jesus praying for you during his life on earth—and continuing to pray for you now? Listen:

[Holy Father],
I do not pray for [my disciples] alone.
I pray also for those who will believe in me

Responding

Just as each of us has one body with many members, and not all the members have the same function, so too we, though many, are one body in Christ and individually members one of another.
(Romans 12:4)

Sit erect. Relax. Close your eyes and take some time to become aware of God breathing life into you. Become aware of God's Spirit in you and the closeness of God to you.

through their word,
that all may be one
as you, Father, are in me, and I in you;
I pray that they may be one in us,....
Father,
all those you gave me
I would have in my company
where I am,
to see this glory of mine
which is your gift to me....
To them I have revealed your name
and I will continue to reveal it
so that your love for me may live in them,
and I may live in them. (John 17:20-21, 24, 26)

Reflecting and Recording

Knowing Jesus prays for me makes me feel...

After reading Jesus' prayer, I would say that he wants
the following for me:

Do I ever ask anyone to pray for me? Do I specify
what it is that I am asking for? Why or why not?

Responding

Choose one or two lines of Jesus' prayer that you
would like to commit to memory. Write them down here:

Sit erect. Breathe consciously and relax. Put yourself
in the Lord's presence. Say your chosen line from Jesus'
prayer, inhaling on the first half and exhaling on the
second half. Close your eyes and repeat this as time
allows. Try to get in touch with Jesus' feeling for you as
he prays these words. Respond in whatever way you wish.

Remembering

Consider what you most need in the coming day. Plan
to ask someone to pray for you—specifying your need.
Repeat throughout the day the sentences of Jesus' prayer
that you committed to memory.

Prayer of Petition

Together: For the Session

Purpose

To better understand prayer of petition

Activity Sheet

21. Prayers of Petition

See Facilitator's Notes, pp. 99-101

Alone: Until Next Session

Prayer Times

1. Scripture and Prayer
2. Putting Ourselves in the Scene
3. Applying Scripture to Life
4. Asking Questions
5. Praying a Psalm
6. Answering Jesus' Questions
7. Praying the Old Testament

Activity Sheet 21

Prayers of Petition

1. It has been said that "Prayer doesn't change God; prayer changes us." What do you think is meant by this statement?

2. If God already knows what is going to happen, should we petition God at all? If you say yes, explain why.

3. What benefits come to *us* by praying prayers of petition?

4. St. Matthew's football team goes into church before the game and prays to win. Meanwhile, St. Mark's team is spending some time in their locker room praying for victory. Do these prayers influence God? Do they affect those who are praying? Should we or should we not pray for these things?

5. What do you think of praying for such things as a parking place, a winning lottery number, a good grade on an exam?

6. What do you think of the belief that prayers will be answered only if we pray a certain prayer for a certain number of days and, conversely, will not be answered if we miss some days or some of the words of the prayer?

7. During the general intercessions at Mass the commentator prays for good weather for the parish picnic. Meanwhile, the farmers in a parish several miles away pray for rain needed for the crops. Discuss the images of God that underlie these prayers? What images of God could result from such conflicts of interest?

8. Some people "bargain" with God. Examples: "If you get me this promotion, I'll put a statue of the Sacred Heart in my yard," or, "If I recover, I'll go to Mass every day from now on." What do you think of bargaining as prayer?

9. Do you know of any examples of when "praying for" someone could be a cop-out for "being an answer to prayer" for the person?

Prayer Time 1

Scripture and Prayer

Relating

Studying doctrine and laws does not of itself ensure healthy, fully alive believers. *Readers Digest* (February, 1988) quoted Samuel P. Gender from *The Washington Post* saying, "If moral behavior were simply following rules, we could program computers to be moral."

For the past several centuries our Church teaching has been focused more on doctrine and less on the Word in Scriptures. While recognizing that doctrine and tradition are important in becoming a Christian, we are returning today to the Scriptures for a richer understanding of God's presence in our daily lives.

The Scriptures reflect the early Christian community's awareness of God's presence. Members' lives were formed by their strong sense of the presence of the Lord in their midst as they listened to the story of Jesus and the letters of their leaders.

We do not want to be religious robots. So we also turn to the Scriptures to give us the lived experiences of the people of God. We want to feel, sense and appreciate God here among us. We want a God we can talk to here and now as did Abraham, David or Peter. The Bible introduces us to this God, and praying with Scripture brings us into God's presence in a special way.

Reflecting and Recording

Go to a quiet place where you can pray and meditate. Make yourself as comfortable as possible and read the following passage from the Bible:

Two men went up to the temple to pray; one was a Pharisee, the other a tax collector. The Pharisee with head unbowed prayed in this fashion: "I give you thanks, O God, that I am not like the rest of men—grasping, crooked, adulterous—or even like this tax collector. I fast twice a week. I pay tithes on all I possess." The other man, however, kept his distance, not even daring to raise his eyes to heaven. All he did was beat his breast and say, "O God, be merciful to me, a sinner." Believe me, this man went home from the temple justified but the other did not. For everyone who exalts himself shall be humbled while he who humbles himself shall be exalted. (Luke 18:10-14)

Quiet yourself. Try to rid yourself of all the things that clutter your mind (your work, your worries and so on). Close your eyes for a few minutes and place yourself directly in God's presence. Relax by taking several deep breaths.

Reread the Scripture passage slowly. Don't try to analyze it; just let the words sink in. *Listen.*

Accept any thoughts or feelings that come to you. Don't try to control them. If you have struggles or questions allow them to develop!

Ask yourself: Which person in the reading most reflects me? Why?

What are my reactions, thoughts, feelings about this reading?

Responding

Look at what you have written. Do you feel content with yourself right now? Respond by telling God in your own words how you feel about yourself. Listen for God's response.

Remembering

Choose a line of Scripture which you like. Repeat it often throughout the day, listening to it in your heart.

Prayer Time 2

Putting Ourselves in the Scene

Relating

One way we can use Scripture in prayer is to read a passage and then project ourselves into the event. We become part of the scene by taking on the roles of different characters and noting our responses.

To pray this way we use as many of our senses as possible. We use imagination to re-create the concrete details—sights, smells, sounds—of the setting. We also imagine the inner feelings of the speakers and those who listen. How did they respond? How will *we* respond?

Reflecting and Recording

Choose a quiet place. Get comfortable. Remove yourself from all distractions. Close your eyes, listen to your breathing and be thankful for the life within you. Let the rhythm of your breathing help you to relax for a few minutes.

Read the following Scripture passage:

As [Jesus] stood by the Lake of Gennesaret, and the crowd pressed in on him to hear the word of God, he saw two boats moored by the side of the lake; the fishermen had disembarked and were washing their nets. He got into one of the boats, the one belonging to Simon, and asked him to pull out a short distance from the shore; then, remaining seated, he continued to teach the crowds from the boat. When he had finished speaking he said to Simon, "Put out into deep water and lower your nets for a catch." Simon answered, "Master, we have been hard at it all night long and have caught nothing; but if you say so, I will lower the nets. Upon doing this they caught such a great number of fish that their nets were at the breaking point. They signaled to their mates in the other boat to come and help them. These came, and together they filled the two boats until they nearly sank.

At the sight of this, Simon Peter fell at the knees of Jesus saying, "Leave me, Lord. I am a sinful man." For indeed, amazement at the catch they had made seized him and all his shipmates, as well as James and John, Zebedee's sons, who were partners with Simon. Jesus said to Simon, "Do not be afraid.

From now on you will be catching men." With that they brought their boats to land, left everything, and became his followers. (Luke 5:1-11)

Sit quietly for two or three minutes imagining the details of this scene: the water, the boat, the fish smells, the people. Then put yourself in Peter's place. You are tired from having worked through the night. You are washing out your nets and about to leave when Jesus walks up, asks if he can climb into your boat, and talks to the crowd of people from it. Sense their reactions! You are also caught up by his words and his eyes!

Now he tells you to go out again to fish! How do you feel? Can you respond as Peter did: "Master, I've fished all night and caught nothing, but if you say so, I'll try again"?

Your catch is so large you need help! How do you feel? What are your reactions?

Jesus says to you, "Follow me." Write your response to this call.

When before this has Jesus called you? (Be as specific as possible.)

Identify times when Jesus may have called, but you didn't recognize it as his call.

Identify the people in your life who have helped you be more aware of Jesus. In what ways could they be instruments of his call to you?

Responding

Reflect on possible ways you can answer Jesus' call to follow him. Take a few minutes of quiet time allowing yourself to realize his presence. Allow him to call you by name and then, in your own words, respond to his call.

Remembering

During the next 24 hours be conscious of events in your life through which you are being called to follow Jesus. Ask yourself periodically, "For whom can I *be* Christ today?"

Prayer Time 3

Applying Scripture to Life

Relating

Another method of praying with Scripture is reading a text and applying it to ourselves. People who have difficulty trying to place themselves into a Scripture scene are often more comfortable in looking at a reading to see how the words apply to their lives.

It's helpful to experience different techniques. Then we can wisely choose the one that we are most comfortable with and use it until it becomes easy. We can later experiment with other techniques which don't seem as comfortable. We are thus able to expand the variety of our prayer styles.

Reflecting and Recording

We often get so tied up with the anxieties and pressures of a day that we lose our perspective on life. We can blow events out of proportion and spend all our energies on one insignificant situation.

Think of something disturbing that has happened to you recently. Perhaps you are angry with someone. Or perhaps you are frustrated because, no matter how hard you try, nothing seems to go right for you.

Read the following passage:

> They came to Jericho next, and as Jesus was leaving that place with his disciples and a sizable crowd, there was a blind beggar Bartimaeus ("son of Timaeus") sitting by the roadside. On hearing that it was Jesus of Nazareth, he began to call out, "Jesus, Son of David, have pity on me!" Many people were scolding him to make him keep quiet, but he shouted all the louder, "Son of David, have pity on me!" Then Jesus stopped and said, "Call him over." So they called the blind man over, telling him as they did so, "You have nothing to fear from him! Get up! He is calling you!" He threw aside his cloak, jumped up and came to Jesus. Jesus asked him, "What do you want me to do for you?" "Rabboni," the blind man said, "I want to see." Jesus said in reply, "Be on your way! Your faith has healed you." Immediately he received his sight and started to follow him up the road. (Mark 10:46-52)

61

Identify different kinds of blindness in your life.

Responding

Imagine Jesus helping you today, right now, to rid yourself of blindness. Talk to him as your friend. Let him know your feelings. As a true friend, he will listen to your story.

Remembering

Try to see all events and people today with the new sight Jesus gave you in your Scripture prayer. Make a special effort to bring all these "clearly-seen" people back to Jesus at the close of the day when you thank him for "eyes to see."

What causes blindness in your attempt to find Jesus in your life? Is there any specific person, event or circumstance that regularly blinds you to what you want to see?

Prayer Time 4

Asking Questions

Relating

Another way to pray with Scripture is to take a reading and ask *Who*, *what*, *when*, *where*, *why* and *how*. The goal of this pursuit is a total submission of one's life to God's will.

The danger of this technique is that it can become an educational process rather than a prayer. This method is a good one insofar as it helps people change their lives.

Reflecting and Recording

If Jesus asked you, "What do you want me to do for you?," what would you say?

Now, brothers, I do not want to leave you in ignorance about spiritual gifts. You know that when you were pagans you were led astray to mute idols, as impulse drove you. That is why I tell you that nobody who speaks in the Spirit of God ever says, "Cursed be Jesus." And no one can say: "Jesus is Lord," except in the Holy Spirit.

There are different gifts but the same Spirit; there are different ministries but the same Lord; there are different works but the same God who accomplishes all of them in everyone.
(1 Corinthians 12:1-6)

Just as we need to probe deeply to find our true selves, so too we need to search into our lives to reflect on our own special gifts. When we discover our unique talents and use them to better our lives and the lives of others, we come to appreciate the Holy Spirit living within each of us in a unique way.

Our greatest gift is the gift of faith in God's presence in our lives. Only through this gift of the Spirit can we proclaim "Jesus is Lord." Paul tells us also that we all have different gifts to offer and that all gifts are manifestations of the one Spirit who lives within each of us.

What are some of my unique gifts?

How am I using these?

When, where and *how* do I use these gifts for others?

Am I satisfied with how I am using my gifts? *Why? Why not?*

Responding

Thank the Spirit within you for each of your special gifts.

Remembering

Be specially conscious today of your special gifts and talents.

Prayer Time 5

Praying a Psalm

Relating

The Psalms are biblical prayers of petition, adoration and praise. They can also form the basis for other methods of prayer.

One technique is to read a psalm until a thought impresses us. Then we can stop and let that thought develop within us. We can expand on it and apply it to our own life situations. We can ask: "What does it say to me today?"

Another method is to rewrite a particular psalm in our own words. In this way we make it a personal prayer.

Reflecting and Recording

We all wear masks over our true selves. We may want others to think that we are "all together" even when we feel fragile. Or we may want others to think of us as strong, or successful, or courageous, or perfect, or as a special kind of person—no matter how we really feel about ourselves. We may want to be looked to as one who has answers, one who is always responsible, or one who follows the "correct" norms of behavior—or one who is always jolly, or always calm and unruffled.

We can wear our masks so regularly and for so long that we become strangers even to ourselves. Then we have to sort through our masks to find out who we really are, what we really feel, what our genuine limitations are. Psalm 139 tells us that God sees behind our masks and knows us, has always known us, *in truth*.

God knows us *exactly* as we are—what makes us tick, the why and the wherefore of our being. We cannot hide from God even in the very depths of our inner thoughts. This truth, expressed in Psalm 139, is both comforting and frightening.

With your eyes closed, imagine yourself in your favorite place, one where you find peace and security. Read the following verses of Psalm 139 and stop for a while at any line that impresses you.

> O LORD, you have probed me and you know me;
>   you know when I sit and when I stand;
>   you understand my thoughts from afar.
> My journeys and my rest you scrutinize.
>   with all my ways you are familiar.
> Even before a word is on my tongue,
>   behold, O LORD, you know the whole of it.
> Behind me and before, you hem me in
>   and rest your hand upon me.
> Such knowledge is too wonderful for me;
>   too lofty for me to attain.
> Where can I go from your spirit?
>   from your presence where can I flee?
> If I go up to the heavens, you are there;
>   if I sink to the nether world, you are present
>   there.
> If I take the wings of the dawn,
>   if I settle at the farthest limits of the sea,
> Even there your hand shall guide me,
>   and your right hand hold me fast.
> If I say, "Surely the darkness shall hide me,
>   and night shall be my light"—
> For you darkness itself is not dark,
>   and night shines as the day.
>   [Darkness and light are the same.]
>
> (Psalm 139:1-12)

Many of our relationships are superficial, and so we experience life only on the surface. As a result we bring our "surface selves" rather than our true selves into our relationship with Jesus.

How can we get to know ourselves better?

We need to take time to delve into our inner selves. We need to look at our masks and at what is beneath them. We can't rush this process; it is lifelong. But we can begin asking questions of ourselves:

What mask(s) do I wear?

What part of me does this mask hide from others? (For example: feeling hurt, needing help, fear of failure, feeling empty, being ordinary.)

Do I also find this part of myself unlikeable or unloveable?

God loves me just as I really am underneath my masks. Can I bring my mask—and what it hides—to God and accept God's love?

Responding

Write a psalm-prayer offering one of your masks—and what it hides—to God. You may wish to follow the format of Psalm 139.

Remembering

As you go about your work or study or leisure today, be aware of God—of Jesus—knowing and loving the you that exists *under your masks.*

Prayer Time 6

Answering Jesus' Questions

Relating

In the Gospels Jesus has a knack of coming directly to the point. His message is always urgent: "You'd better get with it because you never know when your life will be demanded of you."

Jesus also has a way of asking direct questions that call for self-searching. Yet we tend to ignore them, as if they had been addressed to others. The intent of the Gospels, however, is to direct the questions to each of us.

There are about 140 questions asked in the four Gospels. Most of them require more than an easy yes or no answer.

Reflecting and Recording

Meditate on the following passage. Take Jesus' question personally. It is being asked directly of you! Don't pass it off with a quick response—or a response made by someone else.

> Then Jesus and his disciples set out for the villages around Caesarea Philippi. On the way he asked his disciples this question: "Who do people say that I am?" They replied, "Some, John the Baptizer, others, Elijah, still others, one of the prophets." "And you," he went on to ask, "who do you say that I am?" Peter answered him, "You are the Messiah!" Then he gave them strict orders not to tell anyone about him. (Mark 8:27-30)

When Jesus asks, "Who do you say that I am?," the question is not directed to Peter, John or James, but to *you.* You are the modern-day disciple and you now must sit quietly and ponder this question in your heart. To prepare yourself to answer, ask yourself:

When I was a child, who was Jesus to me?

With your eyes closed take three deep breaths slowly and exhale very slowly.

Relax by first telling your legs and arms to become limp. Pause. Now your torso. Pause. Now your head. Turn your head in a circular motion three times.

Jesus is now sitting beside you, and he casually asks: "Who do you say that I am?"

Like Peter you must respond to this question. Peter said that Jesus is the Messiah! To give Peter's answer would be a disappointment to Jesus. He wants your answer. At this point in your life, who is Jesus to you?

When I was a teen or around 20 years old, who was Jesus to me then?

Do you see any change in your perception of Jesus over time?

Finally, what difference does he make in your life today?

Responding

Look over your answers. You may wish to thank Jesus for all he is to you. Or you may wish to search for ways to help increase your understanding of who Jesus is and the difference he can make in your life. Pray in your own words.

Remembering

Whenever you get a few minutes, ask yourself: Who is Jesus to me? Listen to your inner self responding. If possible, jot your ideas down and add them to your responses from this Prayer Time.

Prayer Time 7

Praying the Old Testament

Relating

Several things are helpful when using the Old Testament for meditation. One is some familiarity with the beliefs and customs of the Hebrews. Another is knowing that various forms of literature (for example, history, myths, parables, songs) are present in the Old Testament. The writers also used imagery a great deal because the Hebrew people understood it. Using imagery was part of their way of speaking and writing.

We can read the words of some Old Testament passages in the context of their history and original meanings. Or we can read them as addressed to us today. If we keep this distinction in mind, many readings can become an excellent basis for reflection.

Reflecting and Recording

But now, thus says the LORD,
    who created you, O Jacob, and formed you, O
      Israel:
Fear not, for I have redeemed you;
    I have called you by name: you are mine.
When you pass through the water, I will be with
      you;
    in the rivers you shall not drown.
When you walk through fire, you shall not be
      burned;
    the flames shall not consume you.
For I am the LORD, your God,
    the Holy One of Israel, your savior.
I give Egypt as your ransom,
    Ethiopia and Seba in return for you.
Because you are precious in my eyes
    and glorious, and because I love you.
I give men in return for you
    and peoples in exchange for your life.
Fear not, for I am with you;
    from the east I will bring back your descendants,
    from the west I will gather you. (Isaiah 43:1-5)

Now read this passage again, but replace the words *Jacob* and *Israel* with your own name. Imagine God speaking directly to you.

What do these words mean to you today?

What are some of your greatest dangers?

The Lord says, "Fear not!" What fears do you have?

What, in this passage, does the Lord tell you to do at all times?

Responding

Imagine God saying to you, "You are precious in my eyes. I love you." Get in touch with your feelings and respond to God now in prayer by telling God how you feel as you hear these words.

Remembering

Today, especially if things do not go as well as you expect, repeat God's words to you: "You, N. _____, are precious in my eyes. I love you."

Using Scripture in Prayer

Together: For The Session

Purpose

To learn more about using Scripture for prayer
To experience several ways of praying with Scripture

Activity Sheets

22. Prayer and Temperament
23. Going Deeper Into a Gospel Story

See Facilitator's Notes, pp. 101-103

Alone: Until Next Session

Prayer Times

1. Using Guided Imagery in Prayer
2. Life as a Journey
3. The Kingdom of God
4. Small Beginnings
5. The Community of the Church
6. You Make a Difference!
7. Back to Basics

Also

Pray daily for the person who sat to the left of you at this Session.

Activity Sheet 22

Prayer and Temperament

The following are four types of prayer described in the book *Prayer and Temperament: Different Prayer Forms for Different Personality Types* by Chester P. Michael and Marie C. Norrisey (The Open Door, Inc., Charlottesville, VA).

Ignatian prayer: a way of praying taught by St. Ignatius. We use our imaginations to place ourselves into a story from Scripture. We are spectators at the scene or we become one of the people in the story. Our responses as we do this become the source of our prayer. (Example: the way we prayed the story of Peter and the catch of fish in Prayer Time 2, Session 8. Or the story of the blind man which we prayed together today.)

Augustinian prayer: a way of praying based on the prayers and spirit of St. Augustine. We hear the words of Scripture as if they are being spoken directly to us. (Example: hearing the words of Isaiah 43:1-5 spoken to each of us individually in Prayer Time 7, Session 9.)

Franciscan prayer: a way of praying in the spirit of St. Francis of Assisi. Franciscan prayer is both centered in Jesus (what he felt and did as recorded in the Gospels) and action-oriented. This kind of prayer flows into volunteering at the drop-in center, visiting the lonely at the nursing home, organizing a way to get medical supplies to the tornado victims. Persons who find this prayer more comfortable are the ones who most easily see the suffering and crucified Jesus in the people they serve. Franciscan prayer also flows easily into praise and thanksgiving.

Thomistic prayer: a way of praying named for St. Thomas Aquinas; also called the Scholastic method of prayer. This kind of prayer involves thinking and questioning which usually lead to a resolution. The one who prays takes a passage from Scripture and asks questions such as the following: Who is acting? Why? How does this affect people? When do I fail to heed the message of this Gospel? Where am I most tempted from following Jesus? Ideas follow ideas until the pray-er reaches a logical conclusion or makes a resolution to be followed in life. (Example: Prayer Time 4, Session 9).

Activity Sheet 23

Going Deeper Into a Gospel Story

The following questions can help you go more deeply into the meaning of a Scripture passage or help you relate it to your life. They are meant to be used during a time of prayer when you enter a scene from a Gospel story, become aware of what you are seeing, hearing, smelling and touching and then become one of the characters in the story. Often just one or two of the questions are sufficient to help facilitate your prayer. Each time you use some of these questions in prayer, end with a heart-to-heart talk with Jesus. Respond to his words or actions with your own.

What response was Jesus seeking by what he said or did?

How did Jesus impress the onlookers? How did they react?

What are your reactions to what Jesus said and did? To what the other characters said and did?

What is the most striking characteristic about Jesus that you found in the passage?

What values guided Jesus' choice(s) in this passage?

Does Jesus still want to do today what you see him doing here?

Who is Jesus to you? Does this passage contribute anything to the way you think about him or why you love him?

Do you feel resistance to any part of the passage? Do you feel strengthened or consoled? Bored? Any other feelings?

How does this passage apply to you? What message is the Lord giving you to be lived out in your life?

What might apply to your everyday life: to eating, drinking, sleeping, dealing with neighbors, getting the day's work done?

If you had been present for this incident, what thoughts and feelings would have been with you as you left for home?

What is important about this passage? In other words, why do you think it was chosen to be included as part of God's Word?

Prayer Time 1

Using Guided Imagery in Prayer

Relating

The technique of using guided imagery in prayer appeals to many people. A setting is usually suggested—a quiet place where the pray-er can easily communicate with Jesus or God. People who are not comfortable with the particular place suggested can imagine one that is more suitable.

Reflecting, Recording and Responding

To begin this exercise in one kind of guided imagery prayer, read the following passage:

> What I say to you is: everyone who grows angry with his brother shall be liable to judgment; any man who uses abusive language toward his brother shall be answerable to the Sanhedrin, and if he holds him in contempt he risks the fires of Gehenna. If you bring your gift to the altar and there recall that your brother has anything against you, leave your gift at the altar, go first to be reconciled with your brother, and then come and offer your gift. (Matthew 5:22-25)

Take a few minutes to relax and let yourself be led gently by the following instructions. A series of dots after a phrase suggests that you should pause for awhile.

In your imagination, go to a quiet spot in the park....Find a shady spot under a large tree....

There is a lane in front of you, and Jesus is walking down that lane toward you....Give him time to reach you. He approaches slowly....When he arrives, welcome him and invite him to join you....

When you are ready, tell him of someone with whom you have quarrelled or someone with whom you are not getting along....Tell Jesus all that has happened and how you feel....

Now let Jesus speak to you....Allow him to speak in any manner....

Allow him, now, to forgive you for anything for which you might need forgiveness....Allow yourself to forgive yourself....

Be quiet and listen with your heart....

Open yourself to forgive your brother or sister....

Ask Jesus to give you the courage to do anything you need to do....

Jesus now gets up to leave. Thank him....

See him slowly walk back down the lane, away from you...

Allow yourself time alone with your thoughts...

Now leave this quiet spot and continue with this Prayer Time.

Record any thoughts, difficulties or helps concerning relationships that have come to mind during this time of prayer.

Remembering

As you go through the day be aware of a person you have difficulty relating to. If you can, offer a prayer for that person.

Prayer Time 2

Life as a Journey

(This Prayer Time can serve as a model of prayer for a lifetime. Use it over and over again.)

Relating

An anonymous writer in the Middle Ages spoke of a person's life as a beautiful song. God and the person together sing this song. When someone gets too comfortable in one stage of life and doesn't move onward, the song gets stuck on that particular note.

Each note makes sense because it is part of the entire song. Likewise each event and person has meaning in the context of our entire lives. Life has no meaningless parts. Until life is over, however, we cannot know the full meaning of each happening.

We may not appreciate everything or everybody on the journey of life, but they are part of our song. Everybody—and everything—does reveal God.

God surely doesn't wish for us harsh and bitter events, and there is no easy way to find good in them. Certainly God never wants us to accept passively the evils we face without working to overcome them with good. But God is our constant companion on the journey of life, and God works with us to bring good out of pain, trauma and suffering. Nobody goes through life alone.

God's love can be found eventually in all the experiences of life, even though it may take a lifetime or beyond to realize it.

Reflecting and Recording

> Your ways, O LORD, make known to me;
> teach me your paths,
> Guide me in your truth and teach me,
> for you are God my savior,
> and you I wait all the day.
> Remember that your compassion, O LORD,
> and your kindness are from of old.
> The sins of my youth and my frailties remember
> not;
> in your kindness remember me,
> because of your goodness, O LORD.
>
> Good and upright is the LORD;
> thus he shows sinners the way.
> He guides the humble to justice,
> he teaches the humble his way.
> All the paths of the LORD are kindness and
> constancy
> toward those who keep his covenant and his
> decrees.
> For your name's sake, O LORD,
> you will pardon my guilt, great as it is.
>
> (Psalm 25:4-11)

Look over the events of your life this past week or month or year—whatever it takes to put you in touch with some specific events—positive or negative. List those events with the effects they have had on you. Try to be specific.

Take time to think about the results of these events of your life. Can you find any kind of pattern emerging? How has God been present in those experiences? What changes—positive or negative—occurred?

Responding

Stay with one or two experiences, persons or events from your life. Ask God to help you appreciate how this experience fits into your total journey. Spend a little quiet time in God's presence listening.

Remembering

Try to accept today's events as a part of your journey. Look for Jesus' presence. Keep track of events and, at the end of the day, add them to your journal for future reflection.

Prayer Time 3

The Kingdom of God

Relating

Jesus said over and over that God's Kingdom or God's Reign was the reason he came. He said God's Reign—that is, God's way of life—was completely taking over our world and our lives! Jesus assured us that God's Reign or

Kingdom is the most powerful force in the world and that God's love is renewing and re-creating our world *now*. Is that really possible?

All of us need to pause and consider whether we believe that. Is God's reign of love really coming or not? Is it really—in some sense—already here? How we answer is most important.

> Before all things, however, the kingdom is clearly visible in the very person of Christ, Son of God and Son of Man, who came "to serve and to give his life as a ransom for many" (Mark 10:45).
>
> *(Constitution on the Church)*

To understand God's Reign in our world and in our own lives, we need to understand the person of Jesus. We need to get to know him—how he thinks, who he goes out of his way for, what he gets excited about or angry about, what keeps him going, and so on.

Jesus' death and resurrection is the clearest expression of love we have and, therefore, the clearest picture we have of the effects of God's Reign. In his passion and death, Jesus experienced every evil in this world of ours—a phony trial, lies, betrayal, denial, abandonment, extreme physical and psychological cruelty, political maneuvering. Christ came to a breaking point, yet he remained faithful. He trusted his Father's love, even when he suffered terribly. He did not become embittered; he forgave. Jesus continued to love till the end.

The resurrection of Jesus is the Father's answer to all the evil and blindness in the world. The Father's love is the last word. Accepting God's Reign in our lives means being sensitive to the evils we face but letting God have the last word. *Living God's Reign means consciously choosing to allow God's love to operate in our lives each day.*

Reflecting and Recording

What is the greatest single source of discouragement or frustration in your life?

How does the source of discouragement affect your life on a day-to-day basis? How is it affecting you today?

Is there any possible way that God's Reign could come through this very source of discouragement? If you cannot answer this question clearly, then consider a different one: At this time, can you trust God to bring some good from this—even if you cannot see that good now or in this life?

Responding

> In all this, we are more than conquerers because of him who has loved us. (Romans 8:37)

Sit erect and relax in God's presence. Let yourself be held by him—or her. Imagine the back of your chair as God's hand supporting you. Stay with that. Try to trust in God's power and support of you.

In God's presence and strength, consider your particular source of discouragement. Offer your source of discouragement to God so that God might use it to increase the Kingdom in your life. Listen for any way that God may show you. Or simply place your trust in God to hold you up now.

Remembering

Repeat with conviction throughout your day this simple prayer, "Your Kingdom come!" Note if praying this prayer suggests any action to you.

Prayer Time 4
Small Beginnings

Relating

God's Reign comes! If we take the time to look for the Reign of God and continue to look for it, we will certainly see signs of it. In these prayer exercises, we have been looking at God's ways in each of our lives. Now we need to ask: Do I believe that God is bringing about his Reign through me? Do I believe that my small efforts on behalf of God's Kingdom are needed by God? That God's power in me can do much more than I can imagine?

> The reign of God is like a mustard seed which someone took and sowed in his field. It is the smallest seed of all, yet when full-grown it becomes the largest of plants. It becomes so big a shrub that the birds of the sky come and build their nests in its branches. (Matthew 13:31-32)

The Reign of God comes through significant world events like nuclear arms treaties and the struggles to oppose and reform governments that oppress the poor. Getting involved in social justice issues has to be part of our work to bring about God's Reign. The small mustard seed, however, is the little everyday effort we consciously make to further God's Kingdom. We begin by bringing something—some conscious giving of ourselves to others—and God's power will make it grow.

Reflecting and Recording

As I look over the events of my day, or of the last few days, where can I see God's Reign showing itself?

What can I consciously do or say this day to help God's Kingdom come—in myself, in another, in a situation?

Responding

> To him whose power now at work in us can do immeasurably more than we ask or imagine— to him be glory in the church and in Christ Jesus through all generations, world without end. Amen.
> (Ephesians 3:20-21)

Relax. Sit erect. Spend time centering with the breathing exercise. Then, let your life's breath become God's Spirit being breathed into you. Consciously let that Spirit come deeply into you. In God's presence and power, recall what needs to happen in you today for God's Kingdom to come more fully. Be conscious of God's power in you. Respond to God in any way you choose.

Remembering

Do something specific to further God's Reign today. Write down something you may be able to do.

Prayer Time 5

The Community of the Church

Relating

The great sign of God's Reign on the earth is the community we call church. The love and forgiveness of God are most clearly expressed in the church despite all the mistakes the church makes and all the weaknesses in us, its members. The church is meant to be a model to the whole human race of unity and of concern for others. How we come together as church for each other should light up the world.

> So it is that this messianic people, although it does not actually include all people, and may more than once look like a small flock, is nonetheless a lasting and sure seed of unity, hope and salvation for the whole human race. Established by Christ as a fellowship of life, charity and truth, it is also used by him as an instrument for the redemption of all, and is sent forth into the whole world as the light of the world and the salt of the earth (cf. Matthew 5:13-16). (*Constitution on the Church*, #9)

One clear way for a Catholic to promote God's Reign is to help build the love and the faith of the church community. The church has to become a "we." No matter what hurts or disappointments we have had with the church at the universal level or at the parish level or at the small community level, we are called to work toward creating a more loving and a more faith-filled community.

Reflecting and Recording

Name a person in the church who has been a good influence on you. Explain why.

My greatest difficulty in being a Catholic is...

The one change in me that could help the church be better would be...

Responding

> I pray... that all may be one in us,
> as you, Father, are in me, and I in you;
> I pray that they may be [one] in us,
> that the world may believe that you sent me.
>
> (John 17:21)

Sit erect. Relax. Become aware of yourself in this present movement by using one of the centering techniques. Let yourself hear the Lord call your name, gently and lovingly, again and again. Keep repeating Jesus' words from John 17:21 over and over until these words become your own. This is Christ's last prayer before his passion began. Let this now be your prayer.

Remembering

Repeat the prayer from John 17:21 during the "in-between" times in your day. Note who comes to mind from your small group or the larger church as you pray this prayer.

Prayer Time 6

You Make a Difference!

Relating

Sometimes we accept things because God says so, not because we experience it or see it ourselves. God's Word tells us that each of us does make a real difference in the community of the church whether or not we actually feel that or see it. Can we believe it?

Reflecting and Recording

There are, indeed, many different members, but one body. The eye cannot say to the hand, "I do not need you," anymore than the head can say to the feet, "I do not need you."...If one member suffers, all the members suffer with it; if one member is honored, all the members share its joy. You, then, are the body of Christ.

(1 Corinthians 12:20-21, 26-27)

Your gift—and you do have some gift the church needs—makes a difference. Your struggles to live a life of faith do affect the rest of the community, the big church and your small community. Even your weakness and the acceptance of the forgiveness of the church teaches the church how to forgive. The church is not whole without you.

What is your reaction to the Scripture passage from 1 Corinthians?

Do most people in the church believe they make a difference for the church community? Why?

Is the deliberate restructuring of a parish into small communities (like the one you are in) necessary for the church? Why?

Responding

You are the Body of Christ. (1 Corinthians 27)

Relax. Become centered. Let yourself be present to Jesus Christ who lives in you. Stay in his presence. Hear again his words to you: "You are the Body of Christ." Hear them again. Now bring one other parishioner into your prayer and hear those words again. Now bring someone from your small community who is not particularly close or attractive to you into your prayer. Say, with Christ, his words to this person. End as you wish.

Remembering

Choose some struggle, prayer, action, reconciliation or whatever that you will offer today for the church. Write this down:

Prayer Time 7

Back to Basics

Relating

We began these Prayer Times six weeks ago with this basic belief: God wants to be the closest friend in each of our lives and God speaks in some way through all the events of our lives.

Reflecting and Recording

After doing a centering exercise, read the following aloud, slowly, and repeat several times any phrases that especially attract you:

> For you are my hope, O Lord;
>   my trust, O God, from my youth.
> On you I depend from birth;
>   from my mother's womb you are my strength;
>   constant has been my hope in you....
>
> O God, you have taught me from my youth,
>   and till the present I proclaim your wondrous
>   deeds;
> And now that I am old and gray,
>   O God, forsake me not....(Psalm 71:5-6, 17-18)

This psalm is the prayer of a person who has learned to listen, to notice, to take note of what happens in the events of life and what happens in his or her reactions and feelings.

As we review our days and listen to God in our lives, we may find the following model helpful. We can use all four elements at one time, or we can focus on one of them each evening.

1. *Thanksgiving*: As I recall the day, what and who can I thank God for? Name the events and people. How did these gifts of God affect me?

2. *Contrition*: When did I miss beauty in my day by being closed to events or people or by having a negative attitude toward myself or others? Can I trust God to forgive this in me now?

3. *Petition/Intercession*: As I recall the people I met today and as I pay attention to them now, what need do I see that I may have missed? Or what do I see in myself? Is anything lacking in a relationship? Am I called to intercede for anyone I met from this day? For what?

4. *Resolution*: Am I hopeful as I look to the coming day? In what or whom is my hope founded? What do I resolve to do—or appreciate—or reconcile—this day?

The above model may also be used to review a year—or one's life.

Responding

Relax each part of your body, beginning with the soles of your feet. Put yourself into God's presence and be thankful for the gift of your life right now. Go with the Lord through the past day and relive it step-by-step. Using the model above, review your day from the perspective of thanksgiving, then contrition, then petition. Listen to Jesus at each focus point and respond appropriately. Finally, make your resolve for today.

Remembering

Fulfill today's resolution.

Looking Ahead

Together: For the Session

Purpose

To consider the future of the group

Activity Sheets

24. 'Holy Reading'
25. Deciding About the Future
26. Reflecting on 'Called to Be Church'

See Facilitator's Notes, pp. 103-104

Alone: Until Next Session

Prayerfully consider the future of the group.

Prepare for group celebration.

Use one of the methods of praying with Scripture each day.

Activity Sheet 24

'Holy Reading'

Lectio divina, or "holy reading," is a way of praying with Scripture that St. Benedict made popular as far back as the sixth century. The pray-er does four things: (1) reads a passage of Scripture, (2) reflects on the reading, (3) prays a response that comes from the heart, and (4) spends some time in Jesus' presence.

Part or all of this method of prayer can be adapted and used by people who pray together. The following format offers suggestions.

A. One member of the group opens the Bible to a selected passage and reads it aloud *slowly*, pausing between the phrases. Each person *listens* and notes the words or phrases that strike a chord within.

In silence, each imagines the scene, watches the actions and hears the words *as an observer*. Each person again notes the words or phrases that touch his or her feelings and mulls them over for a time.

After a few moments, the reader says aloud the phrase or word that impressed him or her. After another pause, the next person does the same. This continues around the entire group. No comments are made.

B. Another member of the group reads the same passage—slowly and prayerfully. Each person *listens* again for a word or phrase which "grabs." In silence each enters into the scene—this time *as one of the characters*.

Starting with the reader, one member after another speaks a word or phrase, leaving short pauses of silence between speakers.

C. A third member of the group reads the passage slowly and prayerfully. This time each person places himself or herself in the scene *in relationship to Jesus*, the central figure. Jesus looks at the pray-er. He may speak or just look. If he speaks, what does he say?

Beginning with the reader, each person speaks his or her significant word or phrase again.

D. In a reflective attitude, all share their experiences of the prayer, considering such questions as the following: What particularly impressed me? Did anything touch me? If so, how? How might this passage—or this prayer—influence my life? (Other questions are found on Activity Sheet 23.)

N.B.: All the way through this method of prayer, *no* comments are made and *no* discussion follows any one person's sharing of words or thoughts.

Activity Sheet 25

Deciding About the Future

When people share their faith in the Lord they see more clearly how God is acting in their everyday lives. Sharing faith also helps them see God acting in the church and in the world. Faith-sharing people usually stop thinking of church as a "they" and can say of *themselves* the truth expressed so strongly at the Second Vatican Council: "We" are the church.

Your small Christian community is like the church. You are doing many church activities on a smaller level than the parish does. You are praying together. You are sharing your faith. You are beginning to make connections between your faith and the way you are operating in your family, work and social life.

Do you see your small community having some of the spirit and activity that the parish has?

Your little community could continue to develop as a church if you stay together. You could become one of the Small Basic Christian Communities of your parish.

In a parish with these small communities, the pastoral facilitators of each group meet each month with the pastor or a staff person of the parish. The pastoral facilitator connects his or her small community to the other small communities and to the parish. That way the communities are not just on their own.

The facilitator connects the small community to the parish but each member of the community is responsible for what goes on in the life of that small community. This small church needs each member.

The parish is asking you to consider becoming a small church, a Small Basic Christian Community. With the help of a pastoral facilitator, your community, along with other small churches, would exist within the parish as the most fundamental unit of church.

Until now you have served each other by supporting one another's religious growth. Your community could also be part of something larger. You could become a small community in the church's effort to be the church in smaller groups. You can become part of a deliberate parish plan to bring new life to the Catholic Church.

You are asked to decide whether or not you want to become a Small Basic Christian Community, a base church.

Activity Sheet 26

Reflecting on 'Called to Be Church'

1. How does the experience of your group compare with those featured in the video or described on Activity Sheet 25?

2. How does it make you feel to call your group "a church"? What seems right about this? What seems wrong?

3. In what ways would your group have to grow to become church in the full sense?

4. What can keep these small communities from becoming cliques?

5. What effect might small basic communities like yours have on your total parish? The worldwide church?

SESSION 11

Deciding, Celebrating

Together: For the Session

Purpose

To celebrate together as a faith community
To decide the future of the group

See Facilitator's Notes, pp. 104-105

SESSIONS 1 – 11

Facilitator's Notes

Introduction to Facilitator's Notes

Praying Alone and Together aims to help people pray as a group and as individuals. The specific goals are: (1) to enable people to recognize God communicating to them through their experience; (2) to begin to talk about God in a personal way; and (3) to voice a prayer response in a group setting.

Learning to listen and respond to God is at the heart of small faith communities—and practicing this art is what keeps them from becoming just another study or discussion group. (It's a lot easier to talk about praying than to pray!) We developed this Prayer Module, therefore, precisely to help a group of trusting people reflect more seriously on their lives by praying alone and together.

God works in the everyday as well as in the major events of life—but we have to be paying attention to notice. This prayerful "paying attention" to life is an art that develops with practice. This Prayer Module fosters this art through the private discipline of daily reflection in addition to regular group Sessions for sharing prayer and supporting individual effort.

Getting Started

This prayer workshop was developed at St. Elizabeth Seton Parish in Troy, Michigan, to serve as a "next step" in a plan to restructure our parish into base churches—which we eventually came to call Small Basic Christian Communities. (To learn more about this restructuring process, read the book *Creating Small Faith Communities: A Plan for Restructuring Your Parish and Renewing Catholic Life* from St. Anthony Messenger Press.)

If your parish is already involved in this Called to Be Church process, you and your group have completed phase one and are ready to begin this "next step." A pastoral facilitator has most likely already been selected for your group—and will serve as the guide through this workshop.

If your group is not part of the larger Called to Be Church process, you will need to select someone to serve as facilitator—or decide on a plan for rotating this responsibility. The Facilitator's Notes for each Session are very specific so that no particular expertise is necessary to facilitate a group through this Prayer Module.

Your group will also have to decide on a timetable for meeting. A group may choose to meet every week for 11 weeks or every other week for about five months. We let each group decide what rhythm best suited members' lives. But we found that groups do begin to lose cohesion when the interval between meetings is more than two weeks.

The materials for the group Sessions and the private Prayer Times do not depend on any knowledge of or involvement in the Called to Be Church process. It is only in Session 10 (Looking Ahead) and Session 11 (Deciding, Celebrating) that any reference at all is made to it. In these cases, the facilitator can easily adapt the Plan for the Session to suit the particular nature of his or her small group. At the end of the Facilitator's Notes for Session 11 (page 105), one possible way to continue is suggested for groups not in the Called to Be Church process. It is based on the Review of Life format also found on page 105.

An Overview

Before focusing on any one Session in the pages that follow, familiarize yourself with the various kinds of materials in this book. Read the Preface and look over the Contents.

In the first Sessions of this Prayer Module, listening and responding to God is practiced through listening exercises, praying with imagination, listening to Scripture, going over just one day of one's life. Various Activity Sheets and discussion questions are provided to help the group practice these and other prayer skills.

Many Catholics are not comfortable praying aloud in their own words. For a while, therefore, the group prayer may simply be a quiet time. Being comfortable with the silence is important. Other exercises make shared prayer easier by asking participants to thank God for one gift or to pray for one need or for one person.

Beginning with Session 4, participants are asked to spend 10 minutes a day in some personal reflection or prayer. Prayer exercises to assist participants in these daily Prayer Times are provided. The discipline of daily prayer is stressed and group meetings increasingly depend on individuals spending time in prayer between Sessions.

Not everybody is motivated right away to make time

each day for individual reflection, nor do people easily continue this practice. There also is continuing difficulty in speaking about God in a personal way. Yet, gradually, people do grow in prayer and become more confident that they can pray well as they begin to trust their own experiences.

Prayer does not mean doing all the talking; it can also mean letting a dialogue take place or simply being available to the Lord. Because we don't naturally pray or listen well, the group becomes a great support. Hearing someone we have come to know speak about his or her struggles to be open to God can motivate us to keep trying.

Practical Guidelines

The following tips are offered to make your prayer workshop as helpful as possible:

1. Plan each Session well—and start and end on time. Two hours is a good time limit to set.

2. Plan some social time with simple refreshments at the end of each formal Session. This is an important part of the process, but having the social time at the end allows people the opportunity to continue the sharing or to leave gracefully.

3. The Prayer Module is meant to help each person find his or her own style of prayer. There is no pressure for any participant to pray in any particular way.

4. The dominant or very articulate person can intimidate others if allowed to. If this happens, stop the person as tactfully as possible and ask someone else to share his or her experience. Encourage but don't force members to speak in the Sessions.

5. Breaking into small groups of three or four is critical to the Prayer Module. Generally people share more personally and deeply in a small group. Quieter members speak out more and outspoken members dominate less. Use the small group when the directions call for it.

6. Counting off is the recommended way for breaking into a small group rather than letting people choose the people they are comfortable with. Spouses should not stay together in the small group because they can share with each other later.

7. Give people enough time to complete a writing exercise or to reflect on questions *before* breaking into smaller groups for discussion. Ask members to remain quiet until each person has completed the personal writing or reflection. Never rush people.

8. Specific time directions for periods of silence and sharing are meant to be followed. You may *occasionally* allow a particular discussion to go past the alloted time if it is helpful to the group—and not only to a few individuals.

9. All members, not just the facilitator, should share responsibilities for the group. Different members can host meetings in their homes, prepare refreshments or read a Scripture passage. Some members may even take turns facilitating the Session itself, as long as they are able to stay with the format and style.

10. Remember that you are a member of the group as well as the facilitator. Enjoy the faith and wisdom of the others in the group.

What Is Prayer?

Purpose

To help members of the group

identify their present prayer habits

reflect on the influences on their prayer lives

become familiar with some definitions of prayer

Materials

Journals (Ask each person, ahead of time, to bring a notebook for this purpose.)

Pencils

Plan for This Session

1. Call everyone to a short silence and then to prayer. For example:

We hope that these sessions together will help us to grow in prayer. When the disciples asked Jesus to teach them how to pray, he gave them a model for prayer in the Our Father. Let's recite this prayer together and pledge to each other and to our Father a sincere effort to grow in prayer during these next weeks. Our Father...

2. As this unit on prayer begins, emphasize that prayer is an effort in good communication, not a ticket to good feeling. Read the following slowly and thoughtfully:

"Am I doing it right?" When people ask about praying in the "right" way, they are often assuming that "good" prayer will give them a certain feeling or produce certain results. People often think that prayer should make them feel peaceful or happy or uplifted.

We can't judge the quality of our prayer by our feelings. Prayer is our communication in our relationship with God. As with communication in the other relationships of our lives, there will be ups and downs. At times we experience strong emotions; at other times we seem to have little feeling at all.

When we experience "low" times for a while in prayer, we might take some consolation in knowing that even great saints prayed at length without "feeling" anything. They called these times "dry" periods.

Let's also remember that each of us is an individual.

So each of our dialogues with God, our ways of praying, is different. We can't "program" conversations.

This Prayer Module is meant to offer ways to improve our communication skills in prayer. Two important skills in communication are openness and a listening attitude.

3. Ask everyone to turn to Activity Sheet 1 and to answer each question.

When everyone has completed the sheets, divide group members into groups of three each. Ask them to share answers with one another while respecting anyone's decision to remain silent on any particular item. Allow 10 minutes.

Ask them to fill out Activity Sheets 2 and 3. Then invite each person to share some conclusions with the other two people in the group. Allow 15 minutes.

Ask everyone to read Activity Sheet 4 and answer the questions on Activity Sheet 5. Discuss these answers in the same small groups. Allow 10 minutes.

4. Ask group members to bring their journals each week. Explain that writing is a way to reflect on one's experience. Emphasize that anything written in a journal is for the writer only.

Give them time to answer the following questions in their journals: Are any changes necessary in your prayer life? If so, what are they? (Allow four or five minutes.)

Until Next Session

Ask each member to do the following:

Choose the kind of prayer which he or she finds most satisfying and pray in this way for 10 minutes each day. Suggest making any necessary changes in prayer decided upon in the Session.

Record in their journals any specific difficulties experienced in prayer between now and the next Session.

Who Is God?

Purpose

To help members of the group

become aware of their images of God

move toward deeper personal relationships with God

Materials

"Lord, Teach Us to Pray" (album: *A New Day*) by Joe Wise. Or use any gentle song with easily understood words about our relationship with God.

Record or audiocasette player

Bible

Plan for This Session

1. Introduce listening to a song as a way of praying. For example:

> Listen to the words of this song and meditate on them. Relax as much as you are able and remember that you are in God's presence. Enjoy the time with God. Let God speak to you in the words of the song.

> Play "Lord, Teach Us to Pray" (or other selected song), and then give the group a minute of silence.

2. Ask everyone to fill out Activity Sheets 6 and 7. Then ask them to count off into smaller groups of three or four to share any new insights. Allow 10 minutes for discussion.

> Ask members of the group to take out their journals and answer the following questions: (1) What effect does your description of God have on your prayer life? (2) Do you see a need for any change in your image of God?

3. Read the following to the group:

> Our images of God develop through a long process. A lifetime of events and people have shaped those images.

> All of us can—and should—expand our images of God. As any relationship grows, we change our opinions and perceptions of the other person.

> The way we relate to God is the same way we relate to life. The attitudes that we have toward ourselves and our world are the same attitudes we have toward God. People who don't have any basic regard for themselves, who don't take time to enjoy any pleasures in life, who are not able to forgive themselves for mistakes—these people will have a hard time imaging a close and loving God. People who can't trust the world or other people also find it difficult to trust God.

> The way we live at home every day also affects our relationship with God. If someone's job is highly competitive—even cutthroat—that obviously influences his or her relationship with God.

> But the good news is that *God* breaks through obstacles. We see many examples of people from tough backgrounds who *do* discover God as a loving,

personal friend. Just as a negative attitude toward ourselves and the world affects our attitudes toward God, the reverse happens as well. Our growing love of God will increase our love of ourselves and of our world.

> As we listen to someone talk about a person we know, we sometimes change our opinion of the person talked about. Someone who talks about God may affect our image of God. Real knowledge of a person, however, usually comes from experiencing that person. So, relating to God, especially through prayer and reflective listening, changes our way of thinking and feeling about God. It corrects our distortions.

> Invite any comments and then ask the members of the group to fill out Activity Sheet 8. Then ask them to share their responses in their small group. For example:

> Please share your answers in the same small groups in which you shared earlier. Remember that willingness to talk about our own prayer helps motivate others. We also learn more about ourselves as we listen to others, and they learn from us.

> Allow 10 to 15 minutes.

4. Introduce the following prayer experience like this:

> We are going to try a simple experience of prayer—one which arises from our gratitude for God's gifts to us. As a preparation for your prayer, take out your journal again. Head a clean sheet of paper with the words: *God's Gifts to Me.* Try to come up with 20 gifts for which you are grateful.

> Allow 5 to 7 minutes. Then lead the group into prayer with these or similar words:

> Prayer has to become an experience. We can discuss and analyze prayer week after week, but eventually we have to *pray.*

> We will end all of our sessions with some group prayer. We will sometimes pray silently, sometimes aloud. You are never expected to pray aloud unless you wish to do so.

> The only expectation we put on ourselves as a group is that of being open to prayer. Simply to be with God and to know we are with God is good.

> We are now going to begin with one technique for entering into prayer. Close your eyes. Get into a comfortable position. *(Pause.)* Breathe slowly and deeply several times. *(Pause to allow time to do this.)* As you continue, concentrate on your breathing—

going in and out. *(Pause for 30 seconds or so.)*

Hear these words from Scripture as referring to you. *(Read Genesis 2:7 slowly.)*

Let your breath be God breathing life into you. Take the silence of these moments to experience God affirming your life. *(Pause at least one full minute or longer.)*

Thank God for choosing to give you existence. *(Pause one minute.)* Let's open our eyes and thank God together for any gifts of life for which we are grateful. We can thank God silently or aloud.

Pray aloud thanking God for some simple gift as a way of getting the group started. Pause long enough for everyone who wants to pray aloud to do so. Do not leave long silences once people have started.

Our closing prayer will be the Our Father. Let's pray it slowly—a phrase at a time. Our Father...

Until Next Session

Ask members to recall each evening the gifts of the day and write prayers of thanks in their journals.

S E S S I O N 3

Relating Faith and Prayer

Purpose

To help members of the group

understand prayer as an act of faith

appreciate and understand faith as essential to prayer

Materials

Record or audiocassette of "Do You Really Love Me" by Carey Landry (album: *Hi God*) or "Be Not Afraid" by Bob Dufford (album: *Earthen Vessels*). Or use any gentle religious song expressing faith.

Record or audiocassette player

Bible

Plan for This Session

1. To help members of the group quiet down and relax, you might review the breathing exercise from the last Session and close with the following:

Let yourself experience God breathing life into you, choosing you to live. *(Pause.)* Listen to the words of this song with your heart.

Play the selected song. Allow a minute of silence afterward.

2. Ask group members to take up their journals and title a page with the word *Faith*. Then give these directions:

Let any words or phrases associated with the word *faith* drift into your mind. As they do so write them down. Do not censor them or think about them. Just put them down on the paper. Let as many words or phrases come as will.

Allow three minutes. Then either you or a member of the group read the following aloud:

Faith is what keeps people coming back to prayer. Faith is what keeps people trying. Prayer is an act of faith. We pray because we believe that God exists and that God is present for us. God cares. Every time you and I take time to pray, we make an act of faith and, in doing so, our faith can grow.

Questions about praying "right" and having the "right" technique for prayer are not the important questions. The essential question is: *Am I praying?*

3. Ask members of the group to read Activity Sheet 9 quietly and to answer the questions on Activity Sheet 10. Remind them they will be invited to share answers, but only those answers they choose to share. Emphasize the importance of writing something down in answer to each question to clarify one's own understanding.

Direct them to count off into groups of three or four, depending on the total group size. Give 10 to 15 minutes for sharing on these questions.

Ask everyone to remain in the same small groups and do Activity Sheet 11 silently. Then ask them to talk about whatever they are willing to share. Allow 10 minutes.

Call everyone back to the large group and say, for example:

Look at the words you used to describe faith in your journal. Would you now add or delete anything? Take a few minutes to look over the words and phrases with this in mind.

Facilitate a five- to seven-minute discussion about which words and phrases do and do not describe faith.

4. Ask members of the group to answer the following question in their journals: What do you need to do to help your trust in God develop?

Encourage everyone to be as specific and as realistic as possible, listing only what can actually be accomplished. (Mention that this *won't* be shared.)

Suggest referring to this journal entry during the week as part of a daily prayer time.

5. Introduce this prayer experience by inviting everyone to relax and to put questions and discussions out of mind for a while. Lead them as follows:

Close your eyes and try to relax your body. Imagine the tension leaving each part of your body. *(Name some parts of the body and give time to relax each part. Start with the soles of the feet; work up through ankles, legs, etc.).*

Let yourself hear the Lord call your name—gently, with affection. Hear your name called again and again—quietly, lovingly. If your mind drifts, just bring your attention back to hearing the Lord say your name. *(Pause for a minute or so.)*

Hear this Gospel now. *(Read—or have someone else read—Matthew 8:23-27. Allow 30 seconds of quiet.)*

As you hear this Gospel a second time, imagine yourself in the boat. Experience the boat riding up and down the mountains of waves, being tossed about, being swamped. *(Reread the same passage from Matthew. Allow a minute of quiet.)*

Identify anything that has been upsetting your life lately. What people or events unsettle you? Be aware of your feelings—and accept them. *(Pause for two or three minutes.)*

How does it feel to have Jesus asleep in your boat? *(Pause.)* Wake him up now. What do you want to say to him? *(Pause.)* Say it. *(Pause.)* Does Jesus say anything to you? Allow him time. *(Pause for two minutes.)*

Get ready to leave the boat and return to this room. Take a moment to complete your talk with Jesus. Then open your eyes.

6. Lead them into the closing prayer with the following:

Think of some gift, some positive thing, that came to you in this time together—an insight, perhaps, or a chance to look at your own life, a thought that made you feel good about yourself, a challenge. We'll take a few moments quietly in God's presence now. Then I invite you to mention something you want to thank God for. You can do this quietly or aloud.

Close with the Our Father.

Until Next Session

Encourage them to set aside a little time for reflection each day and to try different ways of praying. For example:

Please find a little time each day for some kind of reflection. Today's prayer with the boat in the storm is one way of praying. You may wish to try this way again with other passages from the Gospels. You may wish to spend some time speaking with Jesus about your journal entries on faith. Or you might like to try different approaches to praying.

SESSION 4

Sharpening Listening Skills

Purpose

To help members of the group

recognize silence and listening as necessary for contemplation

Materials

Bible

Plan for This Session

1. Open the session by inviting everyone to be present mentally and emotionally, as well as physically. For example:

Our time together is short. For each of us, different events and persons have already demanded our attention today. It may be hard to put these demands aside and focus completely on being here with each other. But our group works best when each person makes the choice to be here. I know we are all here physically; our bodies are in this room. Yet our thoughts and feelings may be somewhere else.

Remember that being fully present is a conscious decision. So let's take a minute to bring ourselves mentally and emotionally *here*.

Pause for 15 to 20 seconds. Then lead into prayer with the following:

Expect good things to happen because you are here. Jesus promised he would be with us whenever two or three people gather together in his name. We are even more than two or three, and we do come together because we believe in him. So expect something good to happen in our group.

Let's pray for ourselves as a little community. Let's pray for whatever we need to happen in this time together. We'll take a minute of quiet and then anyone who cares to may mention something—a grace or help or gift—that we can use today.

Pause for a minute and then begin with something simple such as, "I'd like to pray that we can enjoy this time together," or, "I pray that we can be a help to each other in some way." Close with a simple "Thank you."

2. Read the following:

Listening is important to any communication, and prayer is communication. Therefore, listening is important to prayer.

In our busy everyday world, we often listen with only one ear. We half-listen.

But if we don't listen well to people in our lives, and if we don't listen well to the feelings inside us, we can bet we don't listen to God very well either. So the emphasis in this meeting is on developing listening skills.

We can all learn to listen better if we are willing to do the *work* of listening. And listening is work.

We will begin with an assessment of ourselves as listeners. Self-assessment needs to be honest so that we can see if and where change is necessary.

Ask members to fill out Activity Sheet 12—the listening assessment. Then divide them into groups of three or four to discuss answers. Allow 10 to 15 minutes. Introduce Activity Sheets 13 and 14:

Don't be discouraged if you find your listening skills are not all that you would like them to be. You are probably already good at many listening skills. Yet we need to assess our weak points so that we can improve.

The next way to move toward our goal of active listening is to look at any barriers we have in front of us or within us. Please turn to Activity Sheets 13 and 14 and look at the two kinds of barriers mentioned. Activity Sheet 13 asks you to look at barriers in our society and in the life-styles we choose. Activity Sheet 14 asks you to consider barriers within yourself.

Begin to list the barriers or obstacles from society. Work on that list together in your small group.

Allow five minutes maximum to list the barriers in our society. Then ask each person to list, in silence, his or her personal barriers on Activity Sheet 14. Ask each small

group to discuss any insights, questions or new information received from doing these Activity Sheets. Give 15 to 20 minutes for discussion.

Ask members to reassemble into one large group. Invite individuals to share one insight on listening learned from these exercises. Encourage them to share personal insights or impressions rather than elaborations on what has been said. While encouraging brevity, allow enough time for everyone who wants to speak.

3. Introduce the Prayer Times component of the Prayer Module which will begin this week. For example:

In the coming six weeks, we will begin putting into practice what we have talked about in our group concerning prayer. From this point on in our book you will find pages for each Session called Prayer Times. They follow the Activity Sheets for each Session. *(Give time to locate the pages.)* Note that there are seven Prayer Time exercises suggested between each time that we meet. These are not prayers to be memorized or prayers written by someone else. Rather they are exercises that offer a variety of suggestions for reflecting on our lives and on what is happening around us.

Please turn to the Introduction to these Prayer Times on page 20. Take time right now to read this silently.

Review the "four R's" structure which will be carried throughout the Prayer Times. Discuss any questions which arise from reading the Introduction.

Go over Prayer Time 1 with the group. Take time with this so group members feel comfortable about what they are being asked to do daily.

Challenge the group members to pray daily even if they meet with difficulty doing so. For example:

Please try to spend at least 10 minutes daily following these prayer exercises. You may enjoy learning to pray in some new ways. Or you may not like the structure of a particular exercise on some days. However, please give each kind of prayer a chance and see what happens.

Do not feel that you must finish one Prayer Time exercise each day. You may wish to stay on one exercise for several days—or even a week. You may wish to repeat some of the exercises. Or you may wish to substitute another kind of personal prayer on some days. Getting through all of the exercises is not important. Praying daily is! Our time together will be deeper and richer because each of us has spent some time in personal prayer each day.

4. Encourage everyone to get into a comfortable position for this Session's prayer experience.

> Close your eyes. Picture yourself alone on a long stretch of beach. The waves sound a rhythmic beat as they roll onto the shore and then flow out again. Stay with the ebb and flow and the rhythmic sounds until your mind is clear. *(Allow 30 seconds.)*
>
> Let us take a few minutes to think over this day: Each event... *(Pause.)* How you felt about it... *(Pause.)* Each person you met... *(Pause.)* Your feelings about him or her... *(Pause. Allow two or three minutes of quiet before going on.)*
>
> Can you find some experience of God in the events of your day? *(Allow a minute or two for this.)*
>
> Talk to God about your day. *(Pause one minute.)*
>
> If anyone wishes, please feel free to share your prayer aloud with the group. *(Offer a brief prayer of thanks or petition or request for forgiveness to get the shared prayer started.)* Close with the prayer of praise to the Trinity, "Glory be to the Father..."

Until Next Session

Ask everyone to turn to Activity Sheet 15 and to look it over for a few minutes. If the group has enough time, discuss some of the rules and attitudes. Invite them to practice these skills in the coming weeks. For example:

> Keep this Prayer Module book in a place where you will see it often—and keep it open to this Activity Sheet. Reread it frequently. Several times a week, practice listening to someone using a few of the rules each time. As you try these principles with your spouse or friend or parent or child or coworker, note that person's responses. See if they are different from the kind you are used to getting.

Remind the group that all its members will be joined in prayer until the next Session as they all spend some time each day with the same Prayer Time exercises.

SESSION 5

Listening to God

Purpose

To help members of the group

> listen to God in all the events of life

recognize group sharing of beliefs and prayer as supportive to faith life

Plan for This Session

1. After welcoming everyone, read the following:

> It is easy to ask someone at the end of a day, "How has your day been?" We can half-mean that question—and half-listen to the answer—or we can really intend the question.
>
> Ask this question of yourself. "What has the day been like for me?" Take a couple of minutes to listen to your own thoughts and feelings about this day. Then I'll ask each of you to relate something that happened in your day or the way you felt about it.

Allow two minutes for reflection. Then begin the sharing by saying something about your day, focusing on the ordinary. After each person has had an opportunity to speak, lead them into prayer with the following:

> One way to begin our prayer together is for each of us to say in a word or two what we need right now. Then our group can pray for that. Someone may need wisdom to make a decision, or patience with a trying situation in the family, or help in being able to forgive. When you speak your need aloud, you give people an opportunity to support you. So let's take a few moments to reflect on what each of us needs right now.

Pause 30 seconds or so. Begin by mentioning something simple, just one or two words, to get the sharing started. End with the Our Father.

2. Invite a discussion of the Prayer Times experienced since the last Session with the following:

> The first thing we are going to do in this Session is to recall our experiences of the Prayer Times since the last Session. Most people find making time—even 10 minutes a day—difficult. As we said last Session, our kind of world does not encourage listening or reflection. So, as we talk about the Prayer Times, feel free to be yourself. Nobody should feel guilty or be put on the spot for not doing the Prayer times this past week. Even if you haven't used the prayer exercises, you are still part of this group.
>
> Speaking about personal prayer may be quite new for you; it is for many Catholics. It may help to know that you don't need to share everything. In fact, no one should *ever* feel pressured to say anything. Saying *something* about your prayer experience, however, can be helpful to others and to you.

Our failures at prayer, our inability to find time to pray, even our lack of commitment to pray—all this can be told when we trust each other enough. Talking about our struggles can sometimes be more helpful than recounting successes—though we need to say and to hear both. In speaking of our prayer, we provide a certain accountability to each other. Who on this planet cares whether you or I take time to be open to God in our everyday lives? This group does.

We are not a prayer group or a Scripture study group, but a small community of the parish whose members help each other to be serious about a relationship with the Lord. This group will work because people are honest and can make the decision to trust each other.

Confidentiality is presumed. Nothing said in this small community may ever be repeated outside the group.

The greatest gift we bring each other is listening. We don't give advice. We can't solve anyone's problems. But each person can share as much or as little as he or she wishes. Don't ask anyone else for more information from your own curiosity, but do feel free to ask questions to clarify what a person has said. Let the other's experience help you to see God more clearly in your own life.

Ask for any comments before breaking into groups of three to four for sharing. Direct each group to turn to this page for the questions. Allow 10 to 15 minutes.

Did you find time for daily prayer? Why or why not?

What was helpful to you in the Prayer Time exercises?

What was difficult for you? Why?

Has the *Remembering* section worked for you? Do you recall something during the day because of your prayer? Is your day any different? *(Encourage honesty. People should feel comfortable in saying that the prayer made no difference to them if that is their experience.)*

Is there some person in your life who has helped you to pray? If so, how? (Given you confidence to pray? Given an example of perseverance or simple faith?)

Has any person affected your experience of prayer negatively? If so, how? Could this negative influence be a barrier to prayer now? Can you think of any way to free yourself from this influence?

3. Prepare the group for this Session's prayer exercise. If possible, dim the lights. Do anything necessary to cut down on the noise: draw drapes or close doors or ask children to be quiet for a few minutes. Lead the members into prayer with the following:

Assume a comfortable position. Breathe deeply several times. Close your eyes. Become aware of your heartbeat. It may help to feel your pulse on the side of your neck. Simply concentrate on your heartbeat for a few minutes. If other thoughts keep coming to mind, don't fight them, but gently bring yourself back to the steady rhythm of your heart. *(Don't rush this. Take a couple of minutes.)*

Put yourself in God's presence. Relax before God. Let each heartbeat be God's voice to you. Hear God's voice with each beat saying, "I want you to live." Just that one sentence over and over again. Keep repeating these words to the rhythm of your heart. *(Give one to two minutes for this.)* Respond silently to God in your own words in whatever way you wish. *(Allow about one minute.)*

Remain quiet in God's presence for a little longer. Take a few moments to become aware of our group here as we are silently present before God. We are here simply to be with God together.

Picture each member of our group. As you remember each person with care, pray silently for him or her. We will allow a few seconds for each person to be remembered.

Call everyone gently back and ask them to open their eyes.

4. Introduce Activity Sheet 16 with the following:

We have each recalled what the day was like and we have listened to each other's accounts. In our prayer together we recognized God's voice in each heartbeat. Both of these exercises can help us to begin to find God at all times—within ourselves and in all the events and people of our lives.

Sometimes we spontaneously become aware of God when we see something beautiful—a tiny baby, a sunset, a flower. Sometimes we automatically look for God because we are in difficulty or we are suffering or afraid.

Becoming aware of God's presence at these times is prayer. Jesus, however, calls us to pray always. He invites us to find God in more and more times and places.

To help you reflect on the situations where you already find God and those where you may need to consciously look for him, turn to Activity Sheet 16 and follow the directions.

When the members are finished, ask them to divide into groups of three and to share one or two statements of insight gained from doing the exercise.

5. Introduce the idea of "desert experiences" for prayer with the following:

In "prayer language" we call a time set aside from normal activity, a time without the distractions—and often without the comforts—of daily life, a "desert experience." The length may be a day, three days, a month, a year or any desired time. We name it a desert experience because we strip ourselves down to the bare essentials of life so that nothing will keep us from facing our inner selves and God.

Some situations in life (such as disability, illness or loss of a job) may strip us of our regular activities, familiar and comfortable surroundings or opportunities of entertainment. But we may also decide to find or make our own desert experiences to deepen our relationship with God. Activity Sheet 17 is about desert experiences. Please read it and answer the questions.

When all have completed the questions, ask them to divide into smaller groups (three or four) for discussion. Give five minutes.

6. Call members back to the large group and ask them to read Activity Sheet 18. When they are finished, read (or say in your own words) the following:

We have met five times. We need the support of one another if we are to continue our spiritual journey. We also need to know what each person wants and expects of the group. So, for about the next 10 minutes, let's tell each other what we think of our time together so far, how our group meeting may be helping each of us, and how it can become even more helpful. Take a minute to think about your answer to this question: What have I come to expect from our meetings together?

After each person speaks, summarize what he or she has said. When all have spoken, review the purpose of the group. For example:

Our group is meant to be a support to people trying to grow spiritually. Just being together with other folks who care about prayer is a support. While many support groups are meeting in our society, very few—and we are among them—meet to support one another's growth in relationship to God.

We need to remind ourselves that group discussion or group prayer doesn't have to be a peak experience. Some meetings may be slow or some prayer distracting. Yet, just being together in God's presence is good. Meeting as a group supports individual effort. Knowing that we'll discuss prayer is a reminder and a spur to pray.

Ask the group members to take up their journals and write answers to these questions: Do you believe that this group is helping you develop a closer relationship with the Lord? If so, how? If not, what stands in the way of it being helpful?

Until Next Session

Spend at least 10 minutes each day using the Prayer Time exercises.

SESSION 6

'Centering' and the Presence of God

Purpose

To help members of the group

begin to learn centering prayer

find ways to develop a keener awareness of the presence of God

Materials

Individual copies of the first six verses of Psalm 139 taken from a modern translation of the Bible

Plan for This Session

1. Invite each person to name—in a few words—the kind of day he or she has had and to say how each feels right now. (Don't rush this exchange.)

Lead them into a centering prayer exercise with the following:

Let's begin with a time of silence. Find a comfortable position. Close your eyes. Try to still the thoughts of anything that has happened before this present moment. *(Pause four or five seconds.)* Try also, for the moment, to shut off planning any future duties. *(Pause briefly.)* Concentrate on the now, on this moment.

One method of entering into the moment is to concentrate on each part of your body. *(Read the following slowly, pausing each time you ask the listener to focus on a new sensation or conjure up a new image.)* Start with the bottom of your feet and feel the sensation in your toes against your shoes. Be aware of your legs, your knees, your hips, your lower body, your shoulders, your arms, your elbows, your hands, your head. Feel the clothes clinging to each part of your body. Feel the chair or floor supporting you. Focus on these sensations until you can feel each part of your body relax. *(Pause three minutes.)*

Become aware of God's presence. God is holding you gently, supporting each part of you. Let yourself rest as the Lord holds you. Trust the Lord. *(Pause one minute.)*

Become aware of your world: your family, your work, your other relationships, your own struggle. Let God hold everything in your world. As each thing comes to mind, feel the Lord embracing or supporting it. *(Pause three or four minutes.)*

Respond quietly now to the Lord in your own words, saying whatever you wish. *(Pause one minute.)*

Please open your eyes. As we look at each other, let's be aware that all of our worlds are linked together. So let's pray out loud now, or silently if you prefer, to the God who brings our worlds together.

Pause for people to formulate their prayer. If no one starts, begin with a simple, straightforward prayer. For example:

Father, you do care for me. Help me to realize more often that I am in your arms.

After all have had an opportunity to voice their prayers, close by saying, "Thank you."

2. Ask members of the group whether they liked this way of praying. Let the pros and the cons come forward. Then tell them that this kind of prayer is meant to place them in the presence of God by a slowing down and a *centering* inside of themselves. They may be glad to know that people get better at this kind of centering prayer simply by doing it.

3. Begin a review and discussion of the Prayer Times since you last met by breaking into groups of three to four and inviting any comments or sharing of prayer experiences. To facilitate discussion, ask members to turn to this page and discuss the following questions:

What was most helpful for your prayer this week?

What was most difficult for you? Why?

Listening to the daily events of our lives as communication from God is called prayer. Does this seem like prayer to you? Why/Why not?

As you did the *Response* sections in the Prayer Times, did you sense God's closeness at any particular time?

Is praying each day having any effect on how you are living? If so, what effect?

Conclude your discussion with the following:

The exercises in these Prayer Times can also make a good review of the day or of longer periods—a year or one's whole life until the present. The basic question is always, "How is God drawing me to a closer relationship through the happenings of my life?" The next question is, "What is my response?"

4. Continue the focus on centering prayer with the following:

As modern Americans we are caught in busy schedules and many demands on our time and emotions. Even when we sit still physically, our insides may still be racing with thoughts of all we have yet to do this day. We are not present to the present moment because we are living the demands of the future or reliving the events of the past. We are going to learn more about centering so that we will be able to concentrate on the present moment with our thoughts and feelings.

Father Vincent Dwyer, author of the Genesis II program, often uses the term *sacrament of the present moment.* He calls us to realize that God is present and speaking to us in this moment, in this experience, right now. Spiritual writers of the West and of the East stress the importance of living in the present. Centering exercises help us to do this.

We have already used some of these exercises in our prayer together. In the beginning, some of these techniques may seem strange or awkward. You may find some more comfortable than others. Use the ones which you find most helpful.

Activity Sheet 19 offers a few of the many possible centering techniques.

Give the members of the group time to read it carefully. Elicit any comments. The following questions may be helpful.

Do you think centering for prayer can be helpful for you? Is it needed?

Is centering a part of the way you were taught to pray? Or is this your first experience of it?

After the discussion is completed, continue with the following:

During the past weeks we have talked about prayer as listening and as noticing. Since centering prayer quiets us down and gets us into the here and now, it helps us to listen and to notice. In centering prayer we say few words, but we make it possible to experience God's presence more fully. We move away from the thoughts and feelings on the surface to go deep into our center to find God's presence in us.

Centering prayer can seem strange because we do so little talking. Often, however, deep communication between persons doesn't take many words. Just being there for somebody else or with somebody else counts for more. God has more opportunity to change us when we are centered in his presence than when we are doing a lot of talking.

Please begin to use the centering techniques on Activity Sheet 19 to begin your daily prayer. We can't know if centering prayer is good for us until we have tried it.

5. Ask members of the group to complete the following statement in their journals: The way I will become more centered in my prayer this coming week is... Give several minutes for writing.

6. Give each person a copy of the first six verses of Psalm 139—or direct them to turn to this page in their books.

O LORD, you have probed me and you know me;
  you know when I sit and when I stand;
  you understand my thoughts from afar.
My journeys and my rest you scrutinize,
  with all my ways you are familiar.
Even before a word is on my tongue,
  behold, O LORD, you know the whole of it.
Behind me and before, you hem me in
  and rest your hand upon me.
Such knowledge is too wonderful for me;
  too lofty for me to attain.

Offer them the following directions:

When we break after these directions, take Activity Sheet 19 and find a quiet place to be alone. Use one of the centering exercises to become aware of God's presence and to relax. (Take whatever amount of time

you need to get centered—even if you don't get to anything else.) After you have become centered, read these verses of Psalm 139 from the Scripture. Reread them several times. Hear them as God speaking to *you*. Then close your eyes and stay with one word or a few words that strike a chord in you.

Repeat the directions clearly, step by step. Allow at least 10 minutes for their prayer. When all have returned, close by asking one person to slowly read a verse of Psalm 139, the next to read the second verse and so on. After all six verses have been read, ask the whole group to read verse one again together.

Until Next Session

Remind them to spend at least 10 minutes a day with one of the Prayer Time exercises.

SESSION 7

Difficulties in Praying

Purpose

To help members of the group

  note some difficulties in praying
  learn to work through their difficulties

Materials

Several copies of today's newspaper—with sports and comic sections removed

Plan for This Session

1. Call the group to quiet—among themselves and within themselves. Invite them to relax and to place all worries aside. After a moment or two of quiet, suggest that they pray aloud for the needs of the group or the world.

2. Read the following to the group:

We often understand a thought or a feeling better when we put it into words. Saying what we think or feel clarifies and completes the experience. That's why we hear people say, "You know, I never realized I was thinking that way until we started talking."

Teachers often report that they learn more than

their students because the material becomes clearer to teachers as they put the lesson into words. Any experience like a vacation or an illness—or any accomplishment like learning to ski or to drive—is completed by talking about it.

Faith experiences or struggles also become more concrete as we talk about them. But to whom can the average Catholic articulate his or her own faith journey? Most Sunday Mass communities are too large for someone to try to express personal faith. Besides, many people at Sunday Mass would not be comfortable with such expressions.

Lots of people talk about religion; few people talk about their own faith. Many of us have never had the opportunity to express how we experience God in our lives. So we may feel awkward or foolish in trying to express our ideas or feelings about God.

Speaking of what we personally believe about God's action in our lives might be embarrassing or out of place at work. We may not even feel comfortable sharing our faith with friends. Yet, saying what we believe can be a great help to believing more deeply.

This little community right here is, for most of us, the only place where we can express what we believe. We know that our faith journeys are being taken seriously here. We make time for them each week.

In trying to find the words to express how we see God in our lives, we cannot say anything wrong; there are no right or wrong answers. We simply put our experiences into our own words. As with many other new things we try, we get better at it by doing it.

Our little faith community here is a great help because we are here to share faith. None of us has to be all-put-together or perfect. We can share our stumbling efforts and our failures—as well as our successes—as we journey together.

Invite comments and then break up into groups of three to four for sharing on this week's Prayer Times. Remind the groups, if you need to do so, that the point is not to give each other advice or to solve each other's problems. Suggest the following questions:

Is it easy or hard to find time and energy each day for these exercises?

In what way did praying the Our Father line-by-line help you?

Did any phrases cause you difficulty? Which ones?

In what ways are you better able to relate to the Our Father now?

If this was not a helpful way to pray for you, can you identify the reason it wasn't?

3. When the small-group sharing is complete, introduce the Activity Sheet for this Session.

Everyone has difficulties in praying sometimes. If we know these difficulties are normal and okay, maybe this will help us to go on and not to give up. Activity Sheet 20 tells us about dryness and other difficulties in prayer. Let's take time to read this now and to see if any of the difficulties listed are ones we experience.

When everyone has finished, ask each person to pair off with someone else to share any insights, thoughts or feelings that came from reading the Activity Sheet. Give five to seven minutes for this.

Read the following aloud:

Discussing difficulties about praying, like discussing difficulties about any human effort, helps us in two ways. First, just knowing that our particular difficulties are normal, and even expected, encourages us not to quit. After all, prayer—like life—is a journey. Stumbling blocks, detours and rough spots are encountered in most journeys. Second, discussing difficulties in a group helps other people know that they are not alone in what they experience, that others also share some of the same problems. People can identify with each other when both the good times and the hard times are shared.

We may feel at times that we have failed in our efforts, but the only real failure is sitting down in the road and giving up the journey.

We are going to go over the 13 difficultes listed on Activity Sheet 20 together. As I read each one, you may wish to make comments. Or you may want to offer some personal experience to make a point clearer.

Read the first difficulty and wait to see if anyone wants to comment. If no one does, you might share some experience of yours to get the group going. Continue with each item, waiting a short time for comments. You might ask a question on some of the points. After reading #7, note again that the purpose of this group is to motivate each other to prayer. After #12, remind them we can't measure our own prayer by someone else's.

Conclude with the following:

Each of us is a different person and each of us has to relate to God as an individual, or prayer will be phony. Thinking one's own prayer is not as good as somebody else's is a trap.

We need to remember, too, that every prayer time is not a time of good feeling or great insight.

Sometimes we may feel that we've wasted the period. Or we may just feel "blah." Over a period of weeks and years, however, the practice of daily or frequent time with God will have an effect on our lives.

Ask the members of the group if they have definite times for reflection each day. Tell them that the great majority of people report that making prayer a regular part of their schedule is important. When they don't set times of prayer, they tend to drift away from it.

4. Introduce the closing prayer. (Have the newspapers at hand.)

Let's get ready to pray together in a new way. We can help ourselves by letting go of all that we have talked about in order to relax and be open to whatever God has to say to us.

Relax. Get comfortable and close your eyes. Listen to the sounds around you. Listen to individual sounds in this room. Listen to sounds coming from outside. Let the sounds enter into you—freely and deeply. Continue this for a while. *(Pause for one or two minutes.)*

You are in the presence of God. Become aware of God's presence. Just let yourself be peaceful in God or before God. *(Pause two minutes.)*

We will try to remain open and ready to listen as we pray from today's newspaper. The presence or absence of God can be found in the events of any day. So open your eyes and take a section of the newspaper. Take it off to a quiet corner somewhere and read it prayerfully in the presence of God. After you have read of an event, ask yourself these questions: What is God saying in this event? How do I think God sees this event? Or how is God absent? The most important question is, "What is my response?" You will have 10 minutes for this prayer.

When you call the group back together, ask the members to sit in a circle.

As a result of our prayerful reading, let's express our thoughts and feelings to God in prayer. We will each put our papers into the middle of our circle. You may want to offer some prayer of thanks or of petition as you do so. If you can, please pray your prayer aloud.

Pause for a minute. If no one has begun, offer a simple prayer like this: "Lord, you don't seem to be in the things I read about. Help me to see you more clearly."

When verbal prayer seems to have stopped, close with the following:

We will end with the Our Father. Let's join hands and pray each line of the Our Father very slowly.

After the prayer, make this point:

Praying with the newspaper may or may not be your individual way of praying. At least you've opened yourself to another possible way to listen to God.

5. Ask each person to take out his or her journal and to list some ways to deal with the "blahs" in prayer. Allow two to three minutes.

Compliment the group, if appropriate, on their honest participation.

Until Next Session

Remind them of the time of their next meeting and of their unity with one another in prayer until then.

SESSION 8

Prayers of Petition

Purpose

To help members of the group

better understand prayers of petition

Materials

A record or tape player

A record or tape of a song about God's love for us and/or our trust in God. Suggestions: "Be Not Afraid" by Dufford; "Only a Shadow" by Landry; "You Are Near" by Schutte (All are published by North American Liturgy Resources.)

A copy of the words to the song for each member

Plan for This Session

1. Open the Session and lead into prayer with the following:

Let's begin by letting each other know something about the day we've had. In a sentence or two, describe your day and how you are feeling right now. First we'll take a few moments to think about the day.

Pause about 20 seconds and, if no one begins, say something about your day. After each person has had an opportunity to speak, continue with the following:

Now let's go over the day in more detail. As you recall this day in your life, remember that God has given it to you as a gift. Try to relax in God's presence. God simply loves you and wants to be with you. We'll pause a little to relax in God's presence now. *(Pause 15 seconds.)*

As you recall your day, think of the people and the events—and of how you were affected by them. We'll take two minutes now to do this. *(Pause.)*

Picture before God each person you met today and pray for what each might need in his or her life. If you spent your day alone, recall your activities and ask God for whatever you need to make your life more filled with love. *(Give two minutes.)*

Let's close now by mentioning the concerns that have arisen from our day or from our world. If you can mention any of these aloud, you will help us all become aware of others, our world, our God.

Pause 10 to 12 seconds and, if nobody starts, begin praying with a phrase such as: "I'd like to pray for..."

2. Begin the review of the Prayer Time exercises with the following:

What is most important in our being together is our honesty with each other. Whatever else happens, each of us has to have the freedom to be himself or herself. As we discuss our Prayer Time exercises, we all need to say what is truly going on in our prayer times rather than to offer some religious-sounding comments that we might think we are expected to say. Remember, we are most genuinely religious when we are being ourselves. If anyone didn't get much from the Prayer Time exercises this week, say just that. We also need to get to any reasons why we didn't have time to pray or why we lost motivation to try. Our focus is on the reason why.

Let's also remember that each person's contribution to the group is in being himself or herself and in trying to pray the exercises between our meetings.

Use the following questions for the discussion. Remind members of the group, if necessary, that they are simply sharing experiences. Advice and problem solving are not appropriate. Break into small groups and allow 15 minutes for sharing.

What was most helpful to your prayer?

What did you find most difficult in the exercises? What difficulties did you find in yourself?

Have you been an answer to someone's prayer recently?

Does the suggestion in *Remembering* help make the entire day more reflective for you? If not, have you found another way to remember God during the day?

3. Introduce the discussion on prayer of petition (Activity Sheet 21) with the following:

Many people have differing views about asking God to give us something or asking God to change something. Some believe in asking for each thing they need or want in their lives. Others do not believe in prayers of petition at all. We are going to discuss some questions which are often raised about prayers of petition. Let's turn to Activity Sheet 21 and look over all of the questions. When you have done that, begin to answer the questions briefly. You can use these notes a little later when we discuss the issues.

Give seven or eight minutes for silent thought and writing. Then take the questions one by one for about 20 to 25 minutes.

Throughout the discussion, safeguard the following points about prayers of petition: (a) God already loves us and cares about us. We do not have to convince God to do either. (b) Bargaining with God, trying to wear God down, *could* reflect low trust in God's love or in one's own loveableness. (c) Trusting in the particular words of a prayer or the number of times a prayer is said is trusting in something other than God. (d) Praying for someone should never be an excuse for not responding to a person's legitimate need and claim on our care. Nor should asking God to change my life be a substitute for taking steps necessary for change.

4. Ask members of the group to take out their journals and write down the following questions:

What is my earliest childhood memory of asking for something?

What is my earliest memory of being ignored or unheard in a request?

Do I feel I can ask another for help in ordinary circumstances?

Can I ask for help in a serious situation?

How would I rate my trust in God in daily living?

Give 10 minutes to write on these questions. Encourage everyone to continue to think about these questions from now until the next Session.

5. Give out copies of the song which will be sung for the closing prayer. Call the group to prayer. As they quiet

down, speak softly. Guide them through the following prayer. (Each pause should last about 10 seconds.)

Find a comfortable position, but sit straight enough not to fall asleep. *(Pause.)* You may wish to close your eyes. Let yourself relax. *(Pause.)* Enjoy this moment. Be aware of the center of your body. Concentrate on your heart. *(Pause.)* Be aware of the Lord in your center. God is right here, present to you, at home in you. *(Pause.)* Hear God speak your name, gently. Hear the Lord say your name with a lot of affection—over and over. *(Pause.)*

Hear God saying to you right now: "Ask and you shall receive; seek, and you shall find; knock, and it shall be opened to you." *(Say these words slowly as you repeat them.)* "Ask, and you shall receive; seek, and you shall find; knock, and it shall be opened to you."

Keep hearing those phrases, or any one of the phrases, over and over again. Don't think too much, but rather go with the rhythm of the words. Let the words carry you. *(Pause one minute.)* Now let your thoughts and feelings go anywhere the Lord leads you. *(Pause one minute.)* Close this time with God by responding in any way you wish. *(Pause 30 seconds.)*

We will end this prayer together by expressing our trust. We do this even though we may feel that our trust is weak. All of us are trying to grow in trust. We are all trying to do so and none of us is alone in that effort. So we will sing this song about trust and try to believe what the words are saying.

Play the song which you selected.

Until Next Session

Encourage the members, as usual, to set aside a certain time each day to do the Prayer Time exercises. Remind them that if time is not set aside, the day usually gets busy and formal prayer time—sometimes even prayer itself—is in danger of being eliminated. The religious quality of our time together depends on each person being a praying individual.

Using Scripture in Prayer

Purpose

To help members of the group

gain more experience in different methods of praying with Scripture

Materials

A Bible for each member

Plan for This Session

1. Before the group assembles, place the chairs in a circle. As people sit down, ask spouses not to sit next to each other. Call everyone to prayer by gently and slowly reading the following:

Take a minute to become quiet inside of yourself. Be sure that you are sitting in a comfortable but not slouchy position. Close your eyes. Begin to relax your body. Start with the soles of your feet and let all the energy and tenseness drain out. *(Pause.)* Relax your ankles. *(Pause.)* Concentrate on the calves of your legs and release any tightness. *(Pause.)* Feel all the tenseness give way in your thighs. *(Pause.)*

Feel the small of your back relax as you let tension flow down and out. *(Pause.)* Let your lower back muscles relax. Continue relaxing each part of your back. *(Pause.)* Imagine someone massaging your neck and shoulder muscles, relaxing all the pressure points. *(Pause a little longer.)* Feel the massaging action at the base of your head. *(Pause.)* Feel it on the top of your head as all the remaining pressure is released from your scalp. *(Pause.)* Enjoy your relaxed and peaceful feeling.

Listen to this passage from Mark's Gospel about the cure of the blind man. As you hear it imagine the noises of the crowd, the smell of the dusty road, the clothing of the people, the way that the blind man looked and felt.

Read Mark 10:46-52 slowly. Then ask everyone to remain with Jesus for a while. Pause for 30 to 40 seconds. Then continue.

Continue to keep your eyes closed and listen to the story again. Keep all the details of the road and crowd and people in mind. Only this time, *be* the blind man—or woman. Experience everything the blind person does. Let Jesus call you over. Answer his question.

Reread the Gospel slowly, but stop after reading Jesus' question: "What do you want me to do for you?" Pause for two minutes and conclude:

Please come back now to our circle and open your eyes. *(Pause.)*

At this time and during the days until our next Session, we are each asked to pray for the intentions of the person who is sitting to our left.

Since each of us is also going to be prayed for, perhaps we could each mention in a word—or a sentence or two—what we most need, what we would like the person on our right to pray for as they hold us before God.

So take a moment to bring to mind some simple need in your life that you are willing to share.

Allow time for this. But if no one starts and the silence gets uncomfortable, begin with something simple such as: "I'm feeling a lot of pressure at work. I need you to pray for me to keep a positive attitude."

Close with the Our Father.

2. Introduce Activity Sheet 22 with the following:

A book called *Prayer and Temperament: Different Prayer Forms for Different Personality Types* suggests that different kinds of Scriptural prayer are more helpful and satisfying to different kinds of people. Four kinds of prayer described in this book are outlined on Activity Sheet 22. Let's look at those right now.

Read and discuss the prayer forms together. Conclude the discussion with the following:

Each of you has found some Prayer Time exercises that are better for you than others. The authors of *Prayer and Temperament* explain why some forms of prayer are more comfortable to some people and less comfortable to others. We don't have time to go into our different personality types right now, but we can understand that it is natural for each of us to have different prayer preferences. Some of you may also want to read the book and perhaps share the information with others who are interested.

3. Introduce Activity Sheet 23 with the following:

Today we read the story of Bartimaeus twice. Recently we also used that story in a Prayer Time exercise. Because the passage is so familiar, we might imagine that we have gotten everything we can get from it. But the Scripture continually invites us to deeper levels of understanding and wisdom, to further lessons in our lives. So we are going to pray with this passage yet another time—and use some of the questions on Activity Sheet 23—to see what further gifts we may receive.

Take a few minutes now to read through and discuss Activity Sheet 23. Then continue.

Now we will each look for a private place and read the story again. Each of us will enter into the scene as we have done before—according to the Ignatian method. We will see the sights, watch Jesus and the other people, hear the sounds and so on. Then we will become one of the characters and move through the scene with the feelings and thoughts that would have been ours had we been the blind man or Peter. This time, however, we will continue our prayer time by using one or two of the questions from Activity Sheet 23.

Ask for any comments or questions. Tell them to turn to Luke 18:35-43 for the story. Ask them to find a place, pray as instructed and return in 15 minutes.

Ask them to break into groups of three or four and use the following to initiate a 15-minute discussion:

Which questions did you use?

Did the questions help? If so, how?

Make a statement, if you can, of one thing you got out of this meditation that you hadn't received before.

Return to large group and ask for further comments or discussion.

4. Ask members to answer the following questions in their journals: What method of praying with Scripture is most helpful to you? How could having a particular method of praying with Scripture help you develop a disciplined prayer life? (Allow three to four minutes.)

5. Begin the closing prayer by leading the group through one of the centering prayer exercises. Then ask each person to concentrate prayerfully on the concerns of the group mentioned in the opening prayer. End with a "Prayer of the Faithful." (As someone mentions a need, he or she should add, "Let us pray to the Lord." Everyone responds, "Lord, hear our prayer.") Ask each one to remember silently the intention of the person in the group that they are praying for. Allow 10 seconds.

Until Next Session

Suggest that some might like to call the person they are praying for this week to assure him or her of prayers. Remind them about praying the Prayer Time exercises daily.

SESSION 10

Looking Ahead

Purpose

To help members of the group

decide the future of the group

Materials

Bible marked at next Sunday's Gospel—or another chosen passage
Video: *Called to Be Church*

Plan for This Session

1. Welcome the members and invite them to become aware of God's presence in the group. Take a minute of silence for this. Then introduce the prayer:

Please turn to Activity Sheet 24. We find here yet another way to pray with passages from the Bible. After we read this we will try the method together for our opening prayer.

After all have had a chance to read Activity Sheet 24, ask for questions or comments. Make sure that everyone understands what the group will be doing. Then follow the format of the prayer using next Sunday's Gospel or some other passsage you have chosen.

2. Ask the members to break into groups of three or four to share anything they wish from their Prayer Time exercises. Any or all of the following questions may be helpful to begin the discussion or to keep it moving. Allow 15 minutes.

What was most helpful to you? Why?

What was most difficult for you? Why?

Could you share any new insights or realizations about the church as the Body of Christ?

Have you made any resolutions or commitments?

Remind the group that no one's experiences or feelings can be right or wrong. We are called to offer one another respectful acceptance.

3. Initiate a discussion of the group's future with something like this:

Today is the second-last Session of our Prayer Module based on *Praying Alone and Together*. We need to consider whether or not we wish to continue meeting as a group to support one another in our faith. One good way to help us focus this discussion of the future is to watch the video *Called to Be Church*.

After the video take five minutes of quiet for each member to answer the questions on Activity Sheet 26. Then discuss the questions. If the video is not available, read Activity Sheet 25 with the group before discussing the questions on Activity Sheet 26.

4. After the discussion, offer the group the following ideas:

If we decide to continue together, we can know that we are not alone. Catholics are gathering in small groups such as ours all over the world. Others, too, know that they need people who care about them, who will help them grow in prayer and in following Christ.

We need to consider how good it is that we can talk about our religion. Outside of this group, how many opportunities would we have to be supported or challenged in our faith? How many opportunities would we have to give support to others?

If we agree to continue together, we will then have two other considerations.

First, how often will we meet? We would have to decide this for ourselves. A truly effective group must meet often enough not to lose its identity, often enough for people to continue to feel each other's presence and support. A month between meetings is a bit long for this. So two hours every two weeks is suggested. If we wish to meet more than twice a month we could do so, of course.

Second, what will we do when we meet? Much the same as we have been doing here. In the first half we would review some of our personal efforts in living as Christians. For this we would use something called a "Review of Life" which consists of helpful questions to keep us in touch with the ways in which we are following Jesus. (See "A Way to Continue" on page 105.)

Initially, we would read a book called *Creating*

103

Small Faith Communities: A Plan for Restructuring the Parish and Renewing Catholic Life. We would read one chapter between sessions and discuss it together when we meet. This will help us further clarify what it means to be a small church and help us work through the various challenges along the way.

Regularly we would pray over the readings for the coming Sunday, especially the Gospel, and connect our own experiences with the experience of the church in those readings. The parish would supply some structured programs at times, perhaps in Advent and Lent.

We would close, as usual, with prayer and a social time.

I want to ask you to think and pray about this until we meet again so that we can discuss what we would like to do. If you have any reactions right now, however, please share them.

5. Ask the participants to answer the following questions in their journals: How has this group been a help to you in developing a closer relationship with God? With Jesus? Do you feel yourself more a part of the parish—and the larger church—because of this small community? Allow three or four minutes.

6. Set a time for the next Session. Since that meeting will celebrate the end of this phase of the group's life and will determine its future, plan some celebration together. The meeting can be planned around a meal, a dessert, or a special kind of snack. Discuss the possibilities and decide.

7. Close by inviting the group to mention simple prayers of petition or thanksgiving. Include not only individual needs but also those of the larger church and the world.

Until Next Session

Ask everyone to use a regular time each day for praying with Scripture from now until the next Session. Remind them that they have models and examples in the Prayer Times and on some of the Activity Sheets.

Deciding, Celebrating

Purpose

To help members

celebrate being together as a faith community

decide on the future of the group

Materials

Food for a celebration

Plan for This Session

1. If possible, begin the sharing in the same room—or even at the same table—where the celebration will take place. Ask each person to make a brief, simple statement about how this group has affected his or her life. Invite each person to name the greatest difficulty experienced in making prayer and the presence of God a part of daily living.

Begin with the following:

Food is a symbol of life. All other gifts are somehow celebrated in a shared meal. So let's first take some quiet time to become conscious of the great gift of life. *(Pause.)* Be aware for a moment of the mystery of yourself, the fact of your own existence. God willed that you should *be*. Thank God. *(Pause.)* Be grateful for the people around this table, people whom God's wisdom has gathered together for 11 Sessions. Let's pray to God—silently or aloud.

Conclude the prayer and invite the group to spend some relaxed time enjoying one another and the food.

2. Invite members to discuss their hopes for the future. Ask people to address the issue of whether to continue on as a Small Basic Christian Community. After everyone has spoken, ask them to come to a decision about the group. Request that a "secretary" write down whatever the members of the group agree to do: for example, meet every other week, set aside a daily time for prayer, pray for each other and the parish and so on. Ask the "secretary" to reread the list to see if everyone agrees. (Ask someone to make a copy to give to each person at the next meeting.)

3. Set a time and place for the next meeting.

4. Close with spontaneous prayers of thanksgiving followed by the Our Father.

A Way to Continue

The Review of Life is one part of the "Two-Hour Format for the Base Church" explained and presented on page 75 of *Creating Small Faith Communities: A Plan for Restructuring the Parish and Renewing Catholic Life* (St. Anthony Messenger Press). It can also be used apart from the larger Called to Be Church process as a way of providing an ongoing structure for any small group that wants to remain together once this prayer workshop is over. Here's how:

Begin each meeting with an opening prayer. (You can draw upon prayer formats introduced through *Praying Alone and Together.*) Then have people break up into twos to share on the following nine questions:

Review of Life

PRAYER/REFLECTION

1. Have I been able to find time each day for some prayer and reflection? If not, what are the barriers?

2. Name an experience of the Lord—or of his absence—in these last two weeks. What did I hear?

3. What was my greatest difficulty in praying since our last meeting?

4. What do I need most to persevere?

ACTION/REIGN OF GOD

5. In what way is my prayer/reflection affecting my family life? Workplace? Society?

6. What challenges am I experiencing in carrying my prayer/reflection into my family, work, society?

CHURCH

7. In what ways am I growing closer to the church, the Body of Christ?

8. In what ways is the Lord calling me to grow closer? Will I respond to his call?

RESOLUTION

9. For the next two weeks, what will be my one, clear-cut and simple plan or resolve? Whom will I ask to pray for me in this regard?

All the questions need not be covered; it is more important to get at the reasons behind a particular response. But discussion should stay to the point, and no lectures or admonitions are ever given!

After a chance for sharing insights with the large group, end the gathering with time for shared prayer. Adding this petition to the group prayer will serve to remind everyone of the point of these continued gatherings:

Lord, help up grow in relationship to you and to all those you send into our lives. Show us the way to help each other toward this goal.

A Bibliography for 'Called to Be Church'

PRIMARY RESOURCES

All available from St. Anthony Messenger Press, 1615 Republic Street, Cincinnati, Ohio 45210 (513-241-5615).

Creating Small Faith Communities: *A Plan for Restructuring the Parish and Renewing Catholic Life.* SBN 977 $4.95.

Praying Alone and Together: *An 11-Session Prayer Module for Small Faith Communities.* SBN 978 $6.95.

Pastoring the 'Pastors': *Resources for Training and Supporting Pastoral Facilitators for Small Faith Communities.* SBN 979 $6.95.

Called to Be Church: *A 28-Minute Introductory Video.* ITM 704 $12.95.

SUGGESTED PHASE-ONE FORMATS:
THE BEGINNING EXPERIENCE

RENEW
For more information contact the Promotion Department, Paulist Press, 997 Macarthur Blvd., Mahwah, NJ 07430. This program can also be used in Phase Two.

Genesis II: *The Original Program in 18 Sessions*
Available at many parish and diocesan media centers, and the accompanying printed materials may be reproduced. Also: The original printed materials are available from The Center for Human Development, P.O. Box 4557, Washington, DC 20017 (202-529-7724). The original movies are available on one videocassette from Tabor Publishing, P.O. Box 7000, Allen, TX 75002. (The current abbreviated form of the Genesis II program offered by Tabor is *not* a useful phase-one format.)

Pathways, Journeys in Spiritual Growth
The Center for Human Development, P.O. Box 4557, Washington, DC 20017 (202-529-7724).

Parish Renewal Weekends
Contact Father Charles A. Gallagher, S.J., Pastoral and Matrimonial Renewal Center, 67 Prince St., Elizabeth, NJ 07208.

SUGGESTED PHASE-TWO FORMATS: THE PRAYER MODULE

Praying Alone and Together
An 11-Session Prayer Module for Small Faith Communities. St. Anthony Messenger Press.

Mark Link's Challenge Program
Includes these three books: *Challenge, Design,* and *Journey.* Available from Tabor Publishing, P.O. Box 7000, Allen, TX 75002.

RESOURCES FOR PHASE THREE: THE BASE CHURCH

For Focus Questions:

Breaking Open the Word of God, by Karen Hinman Powell and Joseph P. Sinwell. Paulist Press.

Serendipity New Testament for Groups. Paulist Press.

Christian Religious Education: *Sharing Our Story and Vision,* by Thomas H. Groomes. Harper and Row. (Note: Difficult reading; intended for educators.)

For Study/Action:

Creating Small Faith Communities, by Arthur R. Baranowski. St. Anthony Messenger Press.

Believing in Jesus: *A Popular Overview of the Catholic Faith,* by Leonard Foley, O.F.M. St. Anthony Messenger Press.

The Story of the Church, *Peak Moments From Pentecost to the Year 2000,* by Alfred McBride, O. Praem. St. Anthony Messenger Press.

The Beatitude Program
A 10-Session Program for Small Groups. Available from The Beatitude Program, 1001 E. Keefe Ave., Milwaukee, WI 53212.

Post-RENEW Resources
Handy booklets on stewardship, peace and justice, the role of the laity, etc. Contact Sheed and Ward, National Catholic Reporter, P.O. 419281, Kansas City, MO 64141.

For Prayer:

Sharing Prayer: *Simple Formats for Small Groups,* by Mary Sue Taylor. St. Anthony Messenger Press.

Praying Alone and Together, by Arthur R. Baranowski with Kathleen M. O'Reilly and Carrie M. Piro. St. Anthony Messenger Press.

Mark Link's Challenge Program. Tabor Publishing.